BECOMING A NEW CHURCH

BECOMING A NEW
Church

Reflections on Faith & Calling

❧

MALCOLM WARFORD

WIPF & STOCK · Eugene, Oregon

Wipf and Stock Publishers
199 W 8th Ave, Suite 3
Eugene, OR 97401

Becoming a New Church
Reflections on Faith and Calling
By Warford, Malcolm L.
Copyright©2000 Pilgrim Press
ISBN 13: 978-1-55635-517-2
Publication date 8/12/2009
Previously published by United Church Press, 2000

This limited edition licensed by special permission of The Pilgrim Press.

To Pam
for the deepest learning

~

In Christ there is a new creation.
—2 Corinthians 5:17

Contents

∼

Acknowledgments

~

I N COMPLETING THIS PROJECT, I recognize my debt to the congregations and seminaries I have served. Congregational life is a crucible in which we are pulled by questions greater than we might conceive and we are invited to be part of people's lives in ways that are surely a gift. Similarly, the communities of faculty, staff, trustees, and students of the seminaries in which I have spent so much of my life have helped me face the possibilities as well as the shortcomings of my own work and calling.

Friends and colleagues have been generous in their willingness to read the manuscript at various stages and share their thoughtful comments with me: Avery Post, Kathryn Neal, Glenn Miller, Gwen Curry, Tom Carson, Verlyn Barker, James Brewer-Calvert, and William MacKay. In addition, Larry Paul Jones, Jerry Sumney, Robin Hicks, Bill Kincaid, Walter Dickhaut, Lee Huckleberry, and Steve Colon have taken time to look at selected essays. In revising and editing the essays at various points, I am grateful for the critical assistance of Mary Baber Reed, Joanna Juzwik McDonald, Denise Goodman, and Janet Beaulieu. Glenna Richardson has processed countless revisions of the text, checked the accuracy of citations, and handled all of these tasks with skill and a sense of humor. In particular, I want to thank Ansley Coe Throckmorton for suggesting this project, Richard Brown for launching it, and Audrey Miller, Timothy Staveteig, and Ed Huddleston for seeing it through.

I am grateful to the faculty and trustees of Lexington Theological Seminary for the sabbatical that gave me time to complete this book. I also want to thank the editors and publishers who first published some of these essays and to express my appreciation for their permission to include them in this book.

In the appendix, a "Colloquy: Questions for Conversation" has been developed for use in congregations. The questions were created with the assistance of Tom Carson and the Inquirers' Group of Pilgrim Congregational Church (UCC) in Anacortes, Washington.

Finally, I want to acknowledge Lilly Endowment, Inc., which made possible research and assistance in writing these essays. In particular, I want to thank Craig Dykstra and Fred Hofheinz for their continuing support and interest in my work.

Introduction

~

T HESE REFLECTIONS ARE written for weary pilgrims and occasional tourists, who are committed to the church as a place of
faith, mystery, and mission, yet are fully aware of how difficult it is
for a local congregation to express this calling. They are addressed
to church leaders who have propped up, patched, and made do for
so long they wonder if there is a future other than more of the same.
I have tried to identify signs of distress, the feelings of loss and sadness, that are found in congregations; most of all, I have attempted
to describe ways of thinking that might lead to a livelier way of seeing and being the church in this twenty-first century.

For liberal Protestants who once assumed a more established
location in the public world, the decline of membership and status
of mainline churches is difficult to comprehend.[1] While there are
still congregations that are growing in numbers, attendance in others is sparse and unpredictable. Many are only a shadow of the kind
of institution they remember. Furthermore, some are so captive to
these images of the past that it is hard for them to conceive of the
church as anything other than a restoration project.

Memory, however, is a tricky thing, and sometimes what we remember is simply the way we wanted things to be. For example,
many of us recall a relatively common Protestant culture in the 1940s
and 1950s that knit together family, church, and community. Sunday school and public school were extensions of each other in those
post–World War II years. Bible readings and the Lord's Prayer began the school day, and many of the public school teachers taught
on Sunday as well. Neighborhoods were communities where people
knew one another by name, and there was a sense that Bethlehem
and Nazareth were just across the county line. Jesus was not a re-
mote figure, but a familiar cultural presence in daily life.[2] On the

other hand, this popular period of Protestant life was a time in which many churches were tested by issues of faithfulness and found wanting. Churches filled to capacity did not as a rule have much room to think about and respond to the cries of injustice voiced in the civil rights movement. A few church leaders and congregations were among the forerunners of the movement for justice, but most were latecomers to the struggle. In fact, our churches reflected the same kind of segregated culture that dominated the whole of society. The churches then, as now, generally followed rather than challenged the status quo. Is this the kind of church we want to reclaim? I think not.

Living now in a pluralistic society, we are tempted to carry over the assumptions of this earlier era. We tend to think that Protestants still occupy the center of public life, and we take for granted the formation in faith that was once taught in places. We know that much of the membership loss in mainline churches comes from the fact that a number of our children walk away from the church. They do not join other churches or religious traditions; they no longer belong to any church. This does not necessarily mean that they are unconcerned about their spiritual lives, but it does indicate that such individual acts of faith are not connected with a local congregation.[3] While there are social reasons for these shifts, at the heart of this alienation is the question of whether the church, especially the liberal Protestant church, expresses a compelling and credible witness to the gospel.

Part of the dilemma facing congregations is that we have tried to sustain an organizational arrangement of multiple boards and committees that has little sense of embodying Christ's ministry. For several generations we have followed an institutional structure that was in many ways inappropriately adapted from the business world. We have lost an understanding of the extent to which the structures of the church's life are forms of ministry. As it becomes increasingly difficult for churches to implement the functional board system we have inherited, basic questions need to be raised concerning the forms of congregational life that call forth commitment and enliven rather than burden those who are called to serve in the life of the church. Before adopting some other model for the organization of the congregation, however, it is critical that we wrestle with substantive issues of faith and calling. My hunch is that the issues of form will come more clearly into view when the questions of mission are made the focus of inquiry within the congregation. In many mainline Protestant denominations, the shape of the future is probably going to be defined by smaller membership congregations. Various factors account for this reality, including declining birthrates among this segment of the population, aging members, the conservative shift in popular religious life, and basic theological issues of faith and mission.[4] The question is, How can we faithfully move into this new era where the assumptions of a privileged place in society no longer function, or they function for only a relatively few congregations? In particular, this raises questions for all of us who are accustomed to seeing institutions defined by membership growth, expanding budgets, and new buildings. With the decreasing presence of these extrinsic measures, is it possible for us to focus on the growth of faith and mission, which may or may not correlate with numerical growth? The gospel is clear on this issue: two or three gathered in Christ's name are sufficient to constitute a community of faith (Matt. 18:20). The essential mark of such a community is faithfulness that more often contradicts rather than confirms standard cultural assumptions.

In this context, Nora Gallagher writes of a church where she came "as a tourist and ended up as a pilgrim."[5] The church she joined had a declining membership, a depressed minister, and a coffee hour where not many spoke to her. But, she affirms, "in the midst of this unhappy place, funny things began to happen": she felt the presence of God, got involved in a soup kitchen, cared for persons she hardly knew, and prayed for the needs of a larger world.[6] Here she found a sense of "interconnectedness, the web of relationships formed in a house where people are trying to keep their souls alive, attempting a resuscitation."[7] In Advent, thinking of her sojourn in the congregation, she concludes, "Tonight I see all our paths converging. Here we are together, in thin space, learning how to breathe."[8]

A local congregation that conceives of its life in this way already knows something about the provisional character of all institutions.

It can initiate projects and develop practices that provide alternatives to the usual ways of doing things. The cost of moving in this direction is giving up our institutional pretensions in order to hear the calling which lies at the deepest roots of church life—that is, to be a community of transformation where the gospel is preached, the traditions of faith are taught, and the members of the congregation are equipped for their responsibilities in the world. Only in reclaiming this vocation can the church renew its form and mission as a faithful institution.[9]

In using the term "renew," I want to be clear that I am referring to what is new in our lives. It is not a matter of restoring or putting things back in place. What I have in mind is a commitment to innovation—trying some things and thinking some thoughts that move beyond the conventions and commonplaces we take for granted. Part of the paradox in thinking this way is that what is actually innovative may not look new at all, and conversely, what sometimes advertises itself as new may turn out to be the same tired thing presented in a glittering and novel package. Robert Grudin has compared innovative thinking to a voyage and characterized such thinking as a kind of exploration.[10] But he also suggests it is "a homecoming, a heroic effort, by individuals exiled in space and time, to realize principles of solidarity and permanence."[11] Christ offers us such solidarity: "Come to me, all you that are weary and are carrying heavy burdens, and I will give you rest. Take my yoke upon you, and learn from me; for I am gentle and humble in heart, and you will find rest for your souls" (Matt. 11:28–29).

At first this invitation appears to be a summons to stop and find a safer place. It seems to echo some of our inclinations to seek shelter in the church we remember from our childhood or to run away from the issues we face. Instead, this invitation is a summons to ministry. Jesus invites us to put aside what weighs us down, and here is genuine rest. When Jesus says, "Learn from me," he is not speaking didactically in terms of passing on information to a passive student. The meaning of these words is closer to apprenticeship than classroom learning.[12] As much as we might like to exit the road to renewal, here Jesus calls us back on the road and offers us companionship for the journey.

In this regard, Luke's Gospel reminds us that it is on the road where many of the most important moments occur for learning the gospel.[13] The story begins on the road to Bethlehem, and it ends, or begins again, on the Emmaus road. It is the road that provides the setting for such stories as the good Samaritan and the prodigal son.[14] The story of Jesus is told not so much as the narrative of settled folk, but of migrants, travelers, transients, who share what they have learned and pass it on to whomever they meet on their journeys. The scene on the way to Emmaus describes weary disciples. They are sad because the story of Jesus did not turn out the way they had anticipated and the crucifixion seems to be the final word. These disciples returned to the road and, in a sense, back to their lives as they were before they encountered Jesus. As they walk along the road, though, they are joined by a stranger who asks them what they are discussing (Luke 24:18). The disciples inquire if he is the only one who has not heard the stories of Jesus' death and the bewildering rumors circulating about his tomb. After the disciples tell as much of the story as they know, they invite the stranger to have dinner with them. In the midst of this meal the stranger reveals himself as Jesus: "When he was at the table with them, he took bread, blessed and broke it, and gave it to them. Then their eyes were opened, and they recognized him; and he vanished from their sight" (24:30–31). As the disciples begin to put together the pieces of what happened, they realize, "Were not our hearts burning within us while he was talking with us on the road, while he was opening the scriptures to us?" (24:32). When the two return to Jerusalem, they find that Simon has seen Jesus as well, and then they tell "what happened on the road, and how he had been made known to them in the breaking of the bread" (24:35).

Although there is no guarantee of safe travel, no clearly marked signs on the road that lies ahead, what we have is the story of Jesus and the shared memory of his presence in our lives. This memory is most of all embodied in hope that follows the pattern of Jesus who took the form of a servant and made us free to live open to the world and its transformation. As T. S. Eliot wrote in the *Four Quartets*:

> This is the use of memory:
> For liberation—not less of love but expanding
> Of love beyond desire, and so liberation
> From the future as well as the past.[15]

The gospel of Jesus Christ is good news; it is a word about who we are as men and women created and redeemed by God. At the same time, we know that we are prone to turn into ourselves and away from God in pursuit of our own interests. This turning toward self is not just a temporary or inconvenient condition; it is our nature. It requires repentance and calls for transformation. In the midst of our humanity, God has acted in Jesus Christ to forgive us and "give us time to amend our lives."[16] This good news is a word of redemption, renewal, and hope. It is out of such hope that we are called to participate in the ministry of reconciliation and to live within the mystery of faith that is explainable only by God's tender mercy. Our lives have been shaped by this gospel, which comes, as Walker Percy once suggested, like the "message in the bottle" arriving on the shores of our lives as "news from across the seas."[17] This message is not our invention; neither is it our accomplishment. It is news that finds us, claims us, points our lives in a different direction from the route we most often follow, and, in the end, brings us home.

Inclined to be tourists, we are called to be pilgrims on this journey in which there is no permanent dwelling except the promise of the new creation that we have seen in Christ (2 Cor. 5:17) and that is described in Revelation as a new heaven and a new earth (21:1–4). We are called to live in the light of this vision that, as Paul Hanson suggests, "continues to be offered to weary pilgrims as refreshment for their souls and sustenance for their spirits."[18]

The reflections included in this collection have been written over many years in the life of the church. Some of them have already been published in other forms, but most have not, and all have been revised for this book. My hope is that they will help us rethink the nature of our situation in liberal Protestant churches in light of our calling as pilgrims, sojourners, and searchers in the community of Jesus Christ.

PART ONE

Describing the Present

~

This present is a resurrection . . . a transfiguration into a world we keep making even when we deny it.
—Northrop Frye, *Creation and Recreation*[1]

ONE

~

The Persistence of Exile

I brought out my baggage by day, as baggage for exile.

—Ezekiel 12:7

We are all exiles . . . God is the only native.

—Andrei Codrescu, *The Disappearance of the Outside*[1]

T HE QUESTIONS THAT OFTEN haunt us as a church are the persisting questions of exile. Removal from a familiar place, dislocation from what can be counted on, and uncertainty about what lies ahead are elements of this sense of loss that so pervades living in a postmodern world that seems to lack any center or depth.[2] For many local churches, this feeling of loss is focused in the emptiness of sanctuaries that now contain only a small fraction of the congregations who once brought life to these sacred places. Sunday after Sunday, lingering remnants of the faithful gather in the assumption that somehow a windfall of cash or a charismatic leader will fill the pews once again. There is guilt about not being able to continue things as they once were. There is anger that others do not join to help turn things around. But most of all, there is sadness as dwindling congregations live in the difficult space between images of the past and dreams of the future.

At its heart, sadness is attached to the loss of what we want. We grieve what is taken from us or what we do not receive. We are disappointed that life does not fulfill our expectations. It is the same with institutions. For example, large parking lots, endowments, easy-to-find locations, and multiple staff are some factors that help congregations increase membership. Many churches, however, do not have such characteristics and numerical growth that depends on

9

these external factors is not much of a possibility. If there are no deeper understandings of the church's growth, then we are caught in the gap between what we want and the mission that lies before us—which may have little to do with numbers at all. It is a recipe for unrelenting sadness. The difficulty is our captivity to standard models. We focus on the apparent success of a few churches without raising the fundamental questions of vocation, that is, who we are called to be and what we are called to do by God. Such questions do not assume that success and faithfulness are related. They call us to issues of fidelity that have the capacity to change our lives.

As long as we see the resolution of our distress in terms of getting our expectations met, then there is no hope; but if we have the capacity to learn in the midst of this moment, then it can be an occasion of resurrection and new life. Along this line, psychoanalyst Elvin Semrad once suggested that "people grow only around sadness. It's strange who arranged it that way, but that's the way it seems to be. . . . It's sad and painful not to have what you want."[3]

In this context, we can understand similar issues facing Israel in the Babylonian exile of the sixth century B.C.E., when Jerusalem was occupied, the Temple was destroyed, and many of the people became refugees. The aching lament of Psalm 137:1 expresses the sense of longing and homesickness felt by the exiles:

> By the rivers of Babylon—
> there we sat down and there we wept
> when we remembered Zion.

At the root of such dislocation is a feeling of sadness that will not go away no matter how much we deny its presence. Often denial takes the form of assuming that this feeling will soon pass, so we gird ourselves to endure for the short while. But then we find that what we had expected to be a limited time seems to have an indefinite tenure, and there is a confusing sense of not knowing whether to settle in or make ready for the road. A fundamental question is, What will we carry with us? The question addresses more than just the issue of necessary provisions; it also asks what kinds of feelings and commitments we will carry. Tim O'Brien, in *The Things They*

Carried, describes soldiers during the Vietnam War: "The things they carried were largely determined by necessity. Among the necessities or near-necessities were P-38 can openers, pocket knives, heat tabs, wristwatches, dog tags, mosquito repellent, chewing gum, candy, cigarettes, salt tablets, packets of Kool-Aid, lighters, matches, sewing kits, Military Payment Certificates, C rations, and two or three canteens of water."[4] But inside, "they carried all the emotional baggage of men who might die. Grief, terror, love, longing—these were intangibles, but the intangibles had their own mass and specific gravity, they had tangible weight."[5]

In a world that does not often show the face of compassion, where is God, and how will we find our way? These are questions addressed in the book of Ezekiel, which describes the experience of exile.[6] We do not know much about this prophetic figure other than he was probably of a priestly family included among the group of leaders who were the first deportees to Babylon. On his way, then, to becoming a priest, Ezekiel was called to be a prophet. In chapter 12, God instructs Ezekiel to show that the Exile is not a temporary inconvenience and that people should prepare for another deportation from Jerusalem. Ezekiel is to convey this warning in symbolic action; he is to enact a one-man show in front of his hut:[7] "Therefore, mortal, prepare for yourself an exile's baggage, and go into exile by day in their sight; you shall go like an exile from your place to another place in their sight. Perhaps they will understand, though they are a rebellious house" (Ezek. 12:3).

Ezekiel might have thought of this command as a logistical issue, that is, How much baggage can I carry on the journey? The issue would then be one of restructuring and rearranging things to fit into a more restricted space. But God shifts the question by instructing Ezekiel to dig through the wall and carry his baggage through the opening. Then God adds, "In their sight you shall lift the baggage on your shoulder, and carry it out in the dark; you shall cover your face, so that you may not see the land; for I have made you a sign for the house of Israel" (Ezek. 12:6). Although not fully understanding what is ahead, Ezekiel responds in faith: "I did just as I was commanded. I brought out my baggage by day, as baggage for exile, and in the evening I dug through the wall with my own hands; I

brought it out in the dark, carrying it on my shoulder in their sight"
(Ezek. 12:7). Since he is told to take only what he can carry on his
back and get through the opening he has dug in the wall, Ezekiel's
limited cargo does not permit him to take the Temple or any of its
appointments. The God who has been bound to the Temple is revealed as the God who will travel with the exiles.

Later on in the story of Ezekiel, the vision of Israel's renewal is
conceived in the now familiar imagery of dry bones coming to life
(37:1–14). It is the promise of return to Jerusalem, but the city to
which many of the people return is not the same city they left. In
this sense, the Exile was not a detour from the journey of faith; instead, it was the major turning point in Israel's relationship with
God and the key to understanding its vocation in the world.

Like Israel, we find it difficult to comprehend how something
filled with such suffering and heartache as the Exile could be a gift
of God. The paradox is that in exile we are offered the chance to
perceive that our calling by God takes us into such exile, not as a
temporary sojourn, but as a way of being in the world. Called by
Christ into a new birth of faith that renews and transforms our lives,
we dare to understand that suffering lies all around and deep within
us. Once our eyes are opened by faith, we see what we dared not
look at before, namely, the continuing reality of sin and suffering.
We live this reality by the hope of the resurrection, which promises
healing, and in the work of reconciliation we are given by God, who
calls the church to be a pilgrim community.[8]

Initially, exile as a way of being in the world might appear to so
focus on the disjunctions in which we live that we are poor witnesses to the joy and energy of God's grace. In fact, the church has
often clothed itself in such grim vestments and seen its witness as
purveyor of harsh and unmerciful instruction. But the irony is that
our recognition of the brokenness of the world and the paradox of
sin and grace in which we live actually permits us to know true joy
for the first time. Instead of joining in the effort to cover up suffering
and rationalize injustice, we can participate in the struggle for justice and peace; we can know that the cost of discipleship is interpreted by joyous knowledge that this is Christ's reconciling work.

The first step in joining this work is recognizing what has to be left behind. Right now we seem to be so preoccupied with packing for the trip that we do not recognize what the journey requires of us. Several years ago, a powerful visual play was enacted off the shores of the New York and New Jersey coastline. Barges filled with the garbage of New York City were prevented from dumping their cargoes into New Jersey waters. For days the New York barges drifted aimlessly up and down the coastline. Eventually, the controversy was resolved by New York taking responsibility for its own refuse problems. But the image of the barges going nowhere is a visual reminder of the problems we face in a church that must decide what it will value and what it will leave behind. This issue faces the structures of the church as we try to discern the priorities and the commitments that will claim us. There is no end to the number of ingenious attempts to fit more into the exilic backpack than it will hold. We do not yet believe that the church is called to a lean and distinctive life without the many props and entitlements that we have assumed in an age of quasi-established status.

Most ecclesiastical organizations are going through their own versions of restructuring. By and large this is the attempt to keep doing what we have always done but with fewer resources. Staffs have been reduced, program units have been downsized, and remaining staff have been given additional titles and responsibilities. On paper many structures look similar to what they have always been, but in their day-to-day functioning, they are not the same at all. The difficulty is that we continue to see the present moment as a temporary matter rather than a time that has its own distinct needs and responsibilities. We have often spoken of this moment as a "time between times." While I think this image has some value, I am more convinced that it may be a means of deluding ourselves about the actual nature of our situation. If we characterize this moment as transitional, then I think there is an unstated conviction that it will soon pass and we will get on to (or back to) a better and more stable time. In contrast, the fact is that we live in an unpredictable world where the "natural laws" we learned in the old science simply do not apply. To find a stable state within the universe described by quantum physics is to dwell in mystery and to know the grace by which we live. It calls us to the continuing creative vocation that is given to us by God.

Part of this vocation is our willingness to explore questions that are not easily answered and trust that within each question there lies, as Mary Caroline Richards suggests, "the steady beat of an answering response" so that "at the same time that we ask what to do, we are doing something."[9] Such questions include the following: Can we leave behind a church consumed by its own survival? Is it possible for us to lay aside expectations that are essentially a demand for the return of a more predictable past? Can we move beyond the murmur of our continuing anxiety about the future long enough to hear the voice of God's calling? Can we live with the realization that, in the end, the only thing we can ever really take with us is our maturity in the gospel and our credibility as witnesses of Jesus Christ?

TWO

~

Memory and Promise

For no one can lay any foundation other than the one that has
been laid; that foundation is Jesus Christ.

—1 Corinthians 3:11

This is the question that the whole ill-gotten-up, arrogantly
ignorant, busy-with-its campaigns-and-cabbages-World asks
halfway up the steps to the Church, "What's in there—anything
worth my time?"

—Carlyle Marney, *Marney*[1]

AS WEARYING AS CURRENT STRUGGLES in the church may be, the
fundamental question facing congregations is how God's presence renews worship, teaching, and mission. This is a matter of recovering what we have left behind as well as an occasion for striking
out into new and unexplored territory. It grows out of the conviction that the light of revelation illuminates our minds, permits us to
see into the recesses of our hearts, and helps us to discern the occasions of God's presence and calling in the public dimensions of our
lives.

As we look around at many churches, however, we find shadows
rather than light, and the emptiness of unused space. In an introduction to a photographic collection of old New England meeting
houses, John Updike writes, "Joy and aspiration have shaped these
churches, but a certain melancholy may fill them . . . these gallant
old shells hold more memories than promises."[2] Even when congregations still gather, the theological and aesthetic vision that designed
these sacred spaces is now often hidden by a jumble of furniture
and artifacts that blur the distinctive lines of a tradition that knew

15

God as light and mystery. In speaking of the vision that created the classic meeting house, Updike suggests, "The New England spirit does not seek solutions in a crowd; raw light and solitariness are less dreaded than welcomed as enhancers of our essential selves. And our churches, classically, tend to seek through their forms, so restrainedly adorned, their essence as houses for the inner light."[3]

Although these congregations often lived in the shadows of their own hearts, their meeting houses had clear windows open to God's light. The appointments within the meeting room were simple and unadorned with the kind of understated design that would not be replicated until the Shakers in another century put hand and heart together. The space helped fashion the souls of those who gathered to hear stories of faith and give thanks to God in prayer and psalms. All of this was possible because this movement of the Spirit sought ways of making contemporary—in visible forms and institutions—the tradition that saw the continuing reform of our lives as the essential practice of faith.

Various theologies, politics, and cultural assumptions were spawned by this New England heritage, but one of the most significant has been the liberal Protestant tradition that influenced so much of our religious and civic life. Centered in piety that was conversant with intellect and respectful of individual initiative and freedom, this liberal tradition believed the church's mission to be centered in public responsibility and reform. As this tradition developed over the years, though, the sovereignty of God became less central to the covenant, and the children of faith increasingly drifted away from the church. In many instances, being liberal became more important than affirming the central tenets of faith, and the expression of religious commitment and spiritual truth was sometimes an embarrassment rather than an expectation in the life of the church. Often, the meeting houses themselves devolved into museums where occasional visitors could see signs of a former vitality.[4]

The novelist Jane Hamilton once commented that the Congregational church in which she grew up was "like the Wonder Bread of religion: You don't have anything substantial to renounce."[5] This is a harsh judgment on the tradition, but not necessarily without truth. In an ironic way, it is precisely the kind of observation that someone raised in any liberal Protestant tradition might be encouraged to make. As I have thought about her words, however, I do not think they convey the whole truth. Anyone who has read Jane Hamilton's novels recognizes the extent to which her writing is profoundly theological. For example, *A Map of the World* is a story of tragedy and forgiveness, an exploration into time and memory that has an essentially Christian understanding of life. At one point, the main character, Alice Goodwin, in the midst of profound suffering (the child she was baby-sitting drowns in her pond) remembers a moment in the past when she and her husband began their life together on the farm that had held such promise. On their first evening at the farm, they swam together in the pond. "At face value," she writes, "it had been a dip on a hot night."[6] But then, reflecting on the nature of that evening, she interprets its meaning: "[It was] something on the order of a baptism, a kind of blessing. It had been impossible to see at the time, to understand what was taking place right under our noses. Without minister and feast and candlelight and absolution, our swim had marked a beginning."[7]

Toward the end of the story, this sense of things is deepened by the recognition that Theresa, the drowned child's mother who had the most right to reject Alice, has actually forgiven her. She knows that "for Theresa, God was something that was outside of her," but for herself, "God was something within that allowed me, occasionally, to see." Theresa had forgiven her "nearly as soon as she thought to blame, so that her forgiveness was allied with what seemed a holy sort of understanding and love."[8]

Earlier in the novel, Alice had wept and prayed in the hospital when Theresa's child died: "Although I had had very little practice," she writes, "the prayer, as crude as an old stick, was surely the genuine article. I could feel the words, feel them crawling on their hands and knees through my hollow bones, clamoring and shouting." At that moment, however, she realized she "had no more tools than a child" and "the obstruction of skepticism."[9] This is the heart of the matter. Perhaps it is not so much that those of us who were raised in similar traditions, like Jane Hamilton, do not have faith. Rather, it is our lack of any language or means of expressing that faith which is the problem. The church tradition that helped form the kind of insight that Jane Hamilton expresses in her work does not provide enough of the framework needed to sustain a continuing practice of faith. We need more than casual forms of nurture. The Puritans' original vision was a holy commonwealth governed by the image of a "city set on a hill." Over time, the commonwealth shrank to the Wednesday evening potluck supper, and the sense of covenant devolved into the folkways of togetherness. Central to this shrinking of purpose and mission was the absence of any serious teaching that sought to shape a distinctive way of believing and being in the world. The church increasingly became a kind of idealized version of what was seen as best in society at large.

As long as the church was the primary social center of middle-class life, congregations could count on a kind of quiet evangelism that gathered an extended family for whom being in church was simply part of their way of life. While this sort of culture is still important in many places, in most of our society it is on the wane as individuals and families find other places where this sense of being together is experienced. In *A Map of the World*, for example, Alice Goodwin suggests that the closest thing to being in church was attending an international folk-dance group with her aunt Kate, which was, "at first glance, nowhere near the Judeo-Christian path to the divine."[10] Each week, "the oddest assortment of people gathered in Ida Noyes Hall and executed dances from the world over. . . . That was our church, our communion."[11]

Here, at least, in the dance group was some feeling of authenticity, an ordered and dependable event, that provided connection and continuity. In not trying to be more than what it claimed to be, the weekly dance sometimes exceeded its calling and was a place of relationship and meaning. In contrast, Alice found the church was a place that often fell below its own self-definition. Called to be a community of love and service, it tended to be closed off by its own prejudices. The minister seemed to be "acting a part, putting on airs he hadn't earned, wearing a solemnity beyond his years."[12]

In comparing the community of the church and the dance group, Jane Hamilton judges the church in predictable and uncomfortable ways. The church comes off as rather hypocritical, while the secular group appears occasionally as a more faithful association. This is a familiar means of justifying our distance from the church out of a sense that the church does an injustice to our own beliefs. Although we may realize that our belief is incomplete and our knowledge only partial, we remain in our own halfway houses so that, over time, what little substance of faith we received as children erodes as we make our way trying to find guidance here and there. A visit to any local bookstore will give us an idea of the persistence of this search in our lives. The self-help, inspirational sections keep expanding as our involvement in institutional forms of faith declines.

Although this sometimes desperate search for meaning is pervasive in our society, it is not often that such seekers turn to churches—especially liberal Protestant churches—as communities that have power to bring forth life. In many ways, the liberal Protestant tradition has gone into the closet. It is a whispered credo among a few at church meetings and even discussed retrospectively over dinner at the American Academy of Religion, but it is not an identity fashionably shared. While theological fashions come and go, it is hard to imagine some kind of bold resurgence of this tradition that once occupied a more central place in religious life. This leaves ex-liberals, who have not already fled to the trendy east side of neoconservatism, somewhere between the often vapid commitments of a weary liberalism and the political maze of postmodernism. For those of us who affirm such liberal commitments as understanding, diversity, and a willingness to consider we might be wrong, the issue is made all the more confusing because seldom are the choices posed in clear-cut alternatives. We live now with a complex array of options that cannot be contained by the old liberal/conservative tags.

The fact is that we are liberal or conservative according to our inclination of the moment. There is little left of the commitment to traditions of thought and practice formed by distinctive principles that could be identified as liberal or conservative. The idea of a tradition that claims precedence over the demands of the moment is not a commonly expressed idea. The possibility that our experience might be shaped intentionally by a way of thinking and acting that we have to learn and practice appears as a far-fetched notion hopelessly out of step with the kind of multiform world in which we live.

As long as influential liberals in church, academy, and various sectors of the public were able to set many of the ground rules for determining the nature of the world, the social task tended to be seen as one of letting others into the club, opening up the rules of admission. But that is not possible anymore, and what is more, it has never really been true. The club has not been as open as imagined. Now there are many clubs, offering contrasting views of the world, just as there have always been, only now this is more obvious. The liberal perspective is just one of many, and not the one that will necessarily evolve into the enlightened view of the majority. Even with better education or a lot of small group discussion, not everyone will agree with the liberal view of things. Living in a world that feels like a marketplace, tempted to become a club, we have the task of moving toward a clearer definition of the church as the community gathered around the story of Jesus Christ. Within this singular confession, however, there must be an affirmation of diverse ways of understanding what this confession means and how it is authoritative for faith and practice. This will not be enough for some Christian traditions, but it is more than what many liberal Protestant churches have acknowledged.

We have tried to be all things to all people, which is a hollow kind of inclusiveness—a vacuous liberalism. Paradoxically, this approach, which is aimed at expressing diversity, often leans toward uniformity shaped by the lowest common denominator. In contrast, as communities gathered in Christ and committed to discerning the divine calling, we can be different from one another because there is a *center* that claims and defines each of us. Without this *center*, there is no unity; neither is there genuine diversity. The difficulty for congregations identified with the liberal tradition is that they have almost no experience of claiming a distinctive identity. Our congregations are filled with people who know what they are against, but they are not sure what they are for, or more to the point, they are for everything without differentiation.

The basic issue is, What authorizes the life of the church? While the creedal churches have been more explicit in centering the nature of this authority in established confessions of faith, the so-called free churches have to claim their own distinctive forms of faith, which constitute a kind of nurturing matrix for congregational life. We are called to practice a distinctive witness to serve Christ that expresses what we stand for and to whom we belong. This is the promise that can transform memory.

THREE

~

Pilgrims and Tourists

To another he said, "Follow me."

—Luke 9:59

When the traveler's risks are insurable, he has become a tourist.
—Daniel J. Boorstin, *Hidden History* [1]

WHEN MEMBERSHIPS DECLINE, congregations often drift into the assumption that their primary responsibility is to maintain the church building. Resources are increasingly committed to housekeeping, and the ministry of the church is essentially defined as caretaking. There are significant reasons for this focus on the building: it is a place of memories, and its rooms are reminders of friends and loved ones. The building is a monument to these lived moments, and so it becomes a repository of past hopes and dreams. In effect, the people of God become curators of a historical site.

In contrast, the primary identity of the church is to be pilgrims, not keepers of the temple, and this identity is the church's essential calling. We know, however, that while we are called to be pilgrims, we mostly act like tourists. In a lot of ways, we are like Macon, in Anne Tyler's novel *The Accidental Tourist*, who writes travel books for people who want to visit foreign cities and "pretend they had never left home": [2] "What hotels in Madrid boasted king-sized Beautyrest mattresses? What restaurants in Tokyo offered Sweet 'n' Low? Did Amsterdam have a McDonald's? Did Mexico City have a Taco Bell? Did any place in Rome serve Chef Boyardee ravioli? Other travelers hoped to discover distinctive local wines; Macon's readers searched for pasteurized and homogenized milk." [3] In its depths, though, the pilgrim's vocation is to be willing to encoun-

22

ter a reality beyond what we already know, to risk the security of ingrained habits, and to resist the urge to run back to the comfort of the familiar.

Over the centuries, the understanding of pilgrimage as a metaphor for the Christian life has been increasingly identified with a kind of antiworldly posture that sees life on earth as a trial through which we must pass to get to a more spiritual world. In this view, pilgrimage tends to become an indulgence in misery and human futility. Such a distorted image of pilgrimage turns us against this world as we await transportation to another.[4]

A renewed understanding of the vocation of the pilgrim begins with the realization that this calling is essentially about keeping our eyes open and our ears alert to the sights and sounds of God's presence. "Pilgrimage experience," writes Richard R. Niebuhr, "deports us from home; it exports us abroad into a hitherto unimaginable reality."[5]

In some corners of the world, the idea of being a pilgrim is nonsense; you cannot be a pilgrim if there is no place to go. If there is no ultimate destination—no larger narrative that interprets our lives—then there is no journey, just a lot of travel. On the other hand, if there is an intentionality about our lives, then it does make a difference the way we live, the decisions we make, and the people we love. The metaphor of pilgrimage acknowledges mystery and admits that our knowledge is incomplete.

For Christians who would be pilgrims, at the heart of the incarnation is the reality that Christ was crucified outside the gate of Jerusalem. The author of the book of Hebrews (13:12–14) makes the point that the reason Jesus died on a cross, in a place considered unclean by the established religious authorities, is precisely to reveal that the church is called to follow him outside the sacred camp. There is no holy place or reservation for the sacred. Christ's faithfulness even to death in the midst of the world is the central image of faith.[6]

In this regard, Helmut Koester indicates, "the distinction is not between 'worldly' and 'unworldly,' or 'outward' and 'inward,' but rather between 'sacred' and 'secular.'"[7] The reality is that we are always in the world, and the question of faith is how we are present in the world and how we perceive the world. In this sense, the church can be as secular as any place in society, and conversely, there are places made sacred even on the garbage heap or in the marketplace. We must discard the dualistic way of thinking that puts the world in one place and the church in another. Instead, we need to conceive of the church as a distinctive presence in the world. We fall into the trap of thinking that we need to make the church a more appealing place for the world. We tend to see the church as the religious sector of the world, whose center and boundaries are essentially defined by status and power outside itself. In contrast, as Christ's body we are called to be a community of faith that challenges the world's customary definition of itself. We are in the world as pilgrims who have seen God's face in Jesus Christ and who are now on the lookout for God's redemptive work in the unfamiliar as well as the familiar places of our lives.

Several years ago, Pam and I were in Japan at the invitation of the Maryknoll Society of the Roman Catholic Church. One day when we were in the old city of Kyoto, Father Emil, the Catholic priest who was our guide, arranged for us to visit a Zen temple and spend an afternoon with a priest and his family. As we waited for the Zen priest to arrive and drive us to his temple, I imagined how he would look: bald, clothed in an orange robe, and wearing sandals or barefoot. Amid my projections, the Zen priest arrived, driving a brand-new Toyota. When he got out, I saw that he had a crew cut and was wearing a red-and-black-checked Maine jacket, the kind supplied by L. L. Bean. On his feet were a pair of Hush Puppies. So much for stereotypes.

Four of us piled into the tiny car—the Zen priest driving, Father Emil at his side, Pam and I in the back. We had not gone more than two or three miles when the Zen priest turned around, smiled, and removed a tape from the glove compartment. He inserted it into the tape deck, adjusted the volume, leaned back, and suddenly the car was filled with the stereophonic sound of Mahalia Jackson singing an old gospel hymn—"I Know God Is Real for I Feel It in My Heart." There for an instant was a world in which cultural distinctions and expectations made no difference at all. As I later discovered, the name of the temple to which we were headed, translated into English, was "The Temple of the Coming Light."

The moment did not result in a new religious movement, and we did not spend time comparing theological perspectives. Instead, after Mahalia Jackson's voice there was silence in recognition that what had happened was more than what could be contained in anything we might say. I felt no need to jump to the conclusion that the Zen priest was actually an anonymous Christian, or that Father Emil was a crypto-Protestant. In fact, I had no idea how they felt about the event other than what I could discern from the shared moment.

As I have thought about that afternoon, I have gradually come to realize that the deepest significance of the event had little to do with me or with Father Emil; rather, it was most of all about the Japanese priest and Pam. During World War II, Pam's father was a navigator on a plane shot down by a kamikaze pilot; he was killed without ever having seen her. Pam knew her father only through old photos, the stories of his life, and the tragedy of his death flying over Manchuria. Here was at least one pilgrim for whom a Japanese priest and the voice of an African American singer were means of grace— and a Toyota the temple of the Holy Spirit. The priest knew nothing of Pam's life, yet that tape played out an act of reconciliation deeper than any words could express.

The church should be a place that makes us ready for such moments and a place for thanksgiving when those moments occur in our lives. The church in this sense is not so much a destination as it is a journey.

A pilgrim's progress is not the trek to some assured happy ending that renders artificial all that has happened along the road. There is real danger on the journey, and there is no foregone conclusion that things will turn out the way we want them to be in this life. Instead, the progress of a pilgrim calls for faith and courage. Along the way we cannot know for sure which persons and what events are occasions of our calling. We are asked only to be ready for those moments.

Although there are no certainties about what lies ahead, there is a promise of another time—a new heaven and earth. There is the assurance that within our time and place there are sightings of what is yet to come and the presence of the One who is that new creation.

The kind of move we are called to make is to define the church in terms of mission rather than as a shrine. Shrines are important, and one of the ministries of a local congregation may indeed be to sustain a building that is a place for worship, but this ministry alone is hollow if it is not founded upon a larger sense of mission. During the worst of the repressive political regime in South Korea in the late 1970s, there was a small congregation in Seoul called the Galilee Church. The congregation was composed essentially of persons who were under suspicion by the government for their protest against the regime's abuse of civil rights. Since the church was not allowed to occupy a building or even legally exist, it moved from place to place each week. To find it, you had to be on the road and involved with those who were trying to work for change in the society. Usually among such people, you could find someone who was part of the church and knew where it was meeting. The church was a movement. There was no church building, not even a steeple; there was only a group of people gathered in Christ's name, which, of course, is a primary definition of the church—a church that has the capacity to move beyond its own weariness. Reclaiming this definition of the church's essential vocation and our calling as the people of God is central to the practice of faith.

PART TWO

Relearning the Gospel

~

Christendom has done away with Christianity, without being quite aware of it. The consequence is that, if anything is to be done, one must try again to introduce Christianity into Christendom.
—Søren Kierkegaard, *Training in Christianity* [1]

FOUR

~

Metanoia

A Way of Thinking

Do not be conformed to this world, but be transformed by the
renewing of your minds, so that you may discern what is the will
of God—what is good and acceptable and perfect.

—Romans 12:2

Metanoia is not an act of the will. It is the unwillingness to
continue. This unwillingness is not an act but an experience.

—Eugen Rosenstock-Huessy, *I Am an Impure Thinker*[1]

IF THE CHURCH IS TO make any significant difference in the world,
it will come leaving behind the assumptions of a worn-out
Christendom in order to relearn the gospel. In its recent past, the
church could survive by seeing itself as a voluntary religious association that relied on some general principles of being sincere and
doing good for others to constitute its core identity. Liberal Protestant churches have generally encouraged a kind of uncritical acceptance of anything anyone wants to believe. In fact, this miscel-
lany of beliefs confirms our liberalism. It also suggests that there is
nothing ultimately worth believing. Even God becomes somewhat
suspect. For us, the idea that there is some common affirmation of
faith that calls us together is not much explored. In the past, we
depended on cultural expectations to bolster church membership;
but now that these expectations no longer function, we find it
difficult to think about the nature of the church or why anyone
should join the church. Thus, we are brought to the fundamental
question of the Christian life and our own commitment to this way
of being in the world.

"Death" and "resurrection," "dying" and "coming to life," are words that have been used to describe the experience of one who takes the name Christian. The question, however, is whether there is any substance to this name when we have such a superficial acquaintance with the traditions of faith. We presume that the residual forms of piety still existing in our society are an adequate understanding of the gospel itself. To a great extent, being a Christian has become just one element in the configuration of ideas that makes up the popular ideal of goodness and the good life in the United States. To become a Christian in this situation is to add one more thing to our lives deemed nice by our culture. There is, therefore, a certain theatricality about the church as men and women participate in a drama that does not quite make sense to them except that in some vague way it makes them feel better. To accept the name Christian in such a setting is merely to put on a cloak of piety that provides a kind of spiritual covering for our established ways of life. Søren Kierkegaard once wrote, "The medium for being a Christian has been shifted from existence and the ethical to the intellectual, the metaphysical, the imaginary; a more or less theatrical relationship has been introduced between thinking Christianity and being Christian—and thus being a Christian has been abolished."[2]

Our continuing colloquies of concern about the state of the church will not begin to deal adequately with the situation until we have the capacity to see that the institutional crisis is a crisis in faith itself. We may look with curiosity toward the evangelical churches and their testimonies of conversion; or in a more secular vein, we may toy with various psychological systems promising change and transformation. But in the end, we must confront the extent to which we have lost sight of the presence of God within our midst and the peculiar power of this presence to help us understand the extraordinary nature of the world we take for granted. The miracle resides in seeing anew the things we have overlooked because of their proximity to us. We can hear with fresh meaning Paul's words in 2 Corinthians 5:17: "So if anyone is in Christ, there is a new creation: everything old has passed away; see, everything has become new!"

Can we believe that this kind of transformation occurs? We may admit that it seems to have happened to other people in various times and places, but we are not entirely sure that it can happen to us. Talk of transformation, or the more traditional term "conversion," leaves us feeling a bit uneasy. We are reminded of revival tents and radio preachers. Images of Jerry Falwell, Oral Roberts, and an army of militant evangelists come to mind. Associated with these images is a feeling of distaste and a sense of extravagance. Since we do not quite dare to think that we may believe, are we not struck in moments of infinite sadness and distress by the very limits we have imposed on our lives? Caught by the clichés of a pseudoscientism, are we not locked into a world robbed of mystery, void of awe, and closed to the possibility of being transformed? The novelist Walker Percy asks, Why do we "feel so sad in the twentieth century?"[3] He questions,

> What does a man do when he finds himself living after an age has ended and he can no longer understand himself because the theories of man of the former age no longer work and the theories of the new age are not yet known, for not even the name of the new age is known, and so everything is upside down, people feeling bad when they should feel good, good when they should feel bad?[4]

The difficulty, of course, is that we are unaware of ourselves. This does not mean that we are not self-conscious in a preoccupying and narcissistic way, but it does suggest that we are not in touch with the larger significance of our everyday lives. The reality in which we live exists for us "as water does for a fish."[5] We do not see it because we take it for granted. What we mean by revelation is an experience of breaking through this ordinary reality by the breaking in of a new reality which transforms our lives.[6]

Within this context, it is important to remember that the purpose of learning is to help us perceive the nature of reality and the purpose for which we live. The origins of the term "education" suggest a movement outward, and this sense of breaking through the medium of our lives and the breaking in of new knowledge and understanding defines the essential nature of learning.

For Helen Keller, the breakthrough occurred on a hot summer day in Alabama when she first apprehended the meaning of a word. She suddenly established a connection with the world and found a possible means of relating to other human beings. At first glance, there might not appear to be any connection between us and Helen Keller. Her experience of learning seems so unique that it has little to do with us who are not blind or deaf. On another level, however, do we not hear without understanding and see without perceiving? Is not our inadequate awareness of ourselves somewhat like Helen Keller's physical limitations? Do we not know the meaning of Percy's "sadness of ordinary mornings"?[7]

As a young child, Helen Keller was stricken by a disease that left her unable to see, hear, and speak. Until the age of seven, she existed with limited ability to communicate with other people and to understand the nature of the world around her. In the spring of 1887, her father employed a special teacher and companion for her, Anne Mansfield Sullivan. Working with Helen Keller throughout that spring, Anne Sullivan taught the young child to spell rudimentary words by making certain finger signs on her palm. But it was a halting, inadequate form of communication. The child still responded in primitive and unpredictable ways to the people and things around her. All of that changed, however, one day in the summer of 1887. A record of that day was later made by Helen Keller herself in the following passage from her autobiography:

> We walked down the path to the well-house, attracted by the fragrance of the honeysuckle with which it was covered. Some one was drawing water and my teacher placed my hand under the spout. As the cool stream gushed over one hand she spelled into the other the word *water*, first slowly, then rapidly. I stood still, my whole attention fixed upon the motions of her fingers. Suddenly I felt a misty consciousness as of something forgotten—a thrill of returning thought; and somehow the mystery of language was revealed to me. I knew then that "w-a-t-e-r" meant the wonderful cool something that was flowing over my hand. That living word awakened my soul, gave it light, hope, joy, set it free! There were barriers still, it is true, but barriers that could in time be swept away.

I left the well-house eager to learn. Everything had a name, and each name gave birth to a new thought. As we returned to the house every object which I touched seemed to quiver with life. That was because I saw everything with the strange, new sight that had come to me. . . . I learned a great many new words that day. I do not remember what they all were; but I do know that *mother, father, sister, teacher* were among them—words that were to make the world blossom for me, "like Aaron's rod, with flowers." It would have been difficult to find a happier child than I was as I lay in my crib at the close of that eventful day and lived over the joys it had brought me, and for the first time longed for a new day to come.[8]

Following her discovery of the term "water," she reentered her home with a sense of joy and hope; yet mixed with those feelings was remorse about her actions in the past: "On entering the door I remembered the doll I had broken. I felt my way to the hearth and picked up the pieces. I tried vainly to put them together. Then my eyes filled with tears; for I realized what I had done, and for the first time I felt repentance and sorrow."[9] The doll she had broken in a fit of anger could not be repaired; it could not be put together again as if nothing had happened. It lay in mute testimony to the past. The world that opened up to Helen Keller, the new universe that evoked a new sense of herself, also allowed her to begin to understand who she had been and the parts of that person which she continued to carry with her. Until she recognized the way in which her previous understandings of the world turned her in on herself and the extent to which she wanted this to be so, little could have happened to bring about such a radical change in her life.

Anne Sullivan's presence made possible Helen Keller's discovery. Anne Sullivan did not cause the learning to occur, but her presence with Helen through all the tedious weeks of dealing with simple signs established a possibility that otherwise would have been missing. She was with Helen as an image of what could be hoped for. Anne Sullivan had no presumptions about her ability to teach Helen Keller, but she knew what settings might be created in which learning could take place. She maintained the continuity of Helen's instruction, and she was ready to be with her when the teachable moment occurred. Furthermore, she understood that the particular breakthrough was a starting point; Helen Keller's education could begin from there.

One way of describing Helen Keller's experience is to see it as an example of what the church has meant by repentance—the kind of learning in which our thoughts are reshaped and our actions informed by a new perception of our lives in relationship to God and the world. The Greek word *metanoia*, "repentance," literally means an "afterthought." In this sense, *metanoia* is a change of mind about some idea or attitude previously held to be true. This change of mind involves emotional as well as intellectual dimensions; it is a shift in perception that is related to a corresponding change of heart, and it assumes a change in behavior as well. It involves admitting we are wrong, experiencing forgiveness, and walking with God in a new direction and with a new sense of being in the world.

When one examines the usage of the term in the Christian Scriptures, it is apparent that *metanoia* is basic to the proclamation of the gospel. For example, Jesus is depicted in Mark as entering Galilee to proclaim, "The time is fulfilled, and the realm of God has come near; repent, and believe in the good news" (Mark 1:15). In the preaching and teaching of Jesus, faith grows out of repentance and confession, and this turning (*epistrophé*) to God is the beginning point of transformation. In Paul's letters, the idea of repentance (*metanoia*) is interpreted as a complete reshaping of our nature and destiny: "Do not be conformed to this world, but be transformed by the renewing of your minds, so that you may discern what is the will of God—what is good and acceptable and perfect" (Rom. 12:2).

In reference to this text, Karl Barth states that "repentance means being open to the strangeness of resurrection and to the free and boundless initiative of faith."[10] It involves our willingness to look again at the hidden places of our lives. If this transformation is to be authentic, he goes on to affirm, we must "steadily refuse to treat anything—however trivial or disgusting it may seem to be—as irrelevant."[11] Barth urges us to engage in "a wide reading of contemporary secular literature—especially of newspapers!"[12] Although everything we do or think is shaped by life in the world, there are points at which, Barth asserts, our thoughts and actions seem "so transparent that the light of the coming Day is almost visible in them."[13] The proclamation of the gospel, repentance seen as transformation, is at the center of education in the Christian life. The apostles were directed to call people to repentance, to baptize them, and to share with them in a common life of prayer and breaking of bread (Acts 2:42). Repentance, then, is the minimal threshold for learning. As such, it is the point of beginning and continuing the renewal of our hearts and minds in understanding the faith and practices of the Christian life. In the early church, persons seeking to belong to the community of faith were required to participate in a period of instruction about the gospel following their testimony to an experience of the risen Christ. The new Christians were introduced gradually to the worship and mission of the congregation. This formation was understood as a process of transformation that involved instruction in the content of the gospel, teaching of the ethical responsibilities expected of Christians, and participation in the life of the community of faith. This constituted the earliest form of learning in the church.

Eugen Rosenstock-Huessy has suggested that "*metanoia* is not an act of will. It is the unwillingness to continue."[14] The wisdom of this definition pushes us toward the recognition that we are not saved by good works or our best intentions. The experience of transformation begins in our unwillingness to continue with our present way of being. By God's grace, we give up the wearisome task of pretending to be what we are not as we admit that we are less than we imagine ourselves to be, yet infinitely more than we thought we could become. This unwillingness is an act of repentance, a change of mind and heart; it is the beginning of the Christian life.[15]

FIVE

~

Hearing and Seeing

Do not remember the former things,
or consider the things of old.
I am about to do a new thing;
now it springs forth, do you not perceive it?

—Isaiah 43:18–19

To the hard of hearing you shout, and for the almost blind you
draw large and startling figures.

—Flannery O'Connor, *Collected Works*[1]

WE BEGIN TO UNDERSTAND the gospel as we recognize that it is
another way of looking at the world; it is not just more of
our own views writ large. Jesus invites us to come to another place,
to head in a different direction, and to see the world as if for the first
time. At the center of the Christian faith is a new word, a voice we
claim is God's, that opens our eyes to perceive the world from a
different vantage point, and in this hearing and seeing to find our
own voice. In a classic description of conversion, Paul relates his
experience on the road to Damascus in terms of hearing, seeing,
and speaking. In Paul's familiar narrative, he hears Jesus calling to
him as he travels toward Damascus: "Saul, Saul, why do you perse-
cute me?" (Acts 9:4). He stops and is struck blind. He can no longer
see the world and is instructed to go to the house of Ananias, where
he is cared for and instructed in the gospel. On leaving Ananias,
Paul sees the world very differently and finds in this seeing a new
way of speaking (Acts 9:1–20). Each of us is called in similar ways to
hear, see, and speak out of our experience of the gospel in our lives.
We often do not respond to this calling because we keep trying to

impose our preconceptions on the gospel and the world—as in the story of Nicodemus.[2] Nicodemus was a leader in the Jewish community. He sought out Jesus to talk with him about questions of faith. He had seen the miracles of Jesus, and he was impressed by the impact Jesus had on the people who followed him. Nicodemus did not doubt that Jesus was a revealer of God. What he wanted was some deeper understanding of Jesus. The conversation begins somewhat like a newspaper interview with Nicodemus taking the lead and obviously expecting Jesus to respond to his questions. The tables, however, are turned immediately by Jesus as he goes to the heart of the matter. Instead of carrying on the interview in Nicodemus's terms, Jesus transforms the interview into a conversation about faith and makes clear the condition for belief is the call to new life: "Very truly, I tell you, no one can see the realm of God without being born from above" (John 3:3). In response, Nicodemus moves to a strangely literal level: "How can anyone be born after having grown old? Can one enter a second time into the mother's womb and be born?" (John 3:4).

Jesus will not get into an argument about the mechanics of birth. He tries to lead Nicodemus to an understanding that the faith he seeks requires him to turn his life around. It is not a matter of seeking an explanation of the realm of God: "Very truly, I tell you, no one can enter the realm of God without being born of water and Spirit.... Do not be astonished that I said to you, 'You must be born from above.' The wind blows where it chooses, and you hear the sound of it, but you do not know where it comes from or where it goes. So it is with everyone who is born of the Spirit" (John 3:5, 7–8). Although Nicodemus hears these words, he does not listen to what they say to him. He looks to Jesus to fulfill his expectations, but he is not able to perceive that in Jesus something new is offered to him. The conversation ends as a standoff. We hear no more of Nicodemus until Jesus' death when he is present on the edge of the resurrection stories.

In contrast with the story of Nicodemus, the story of Jesus and the Samaritan woman (John 4:7–42) leads us to an understanding of the movement of faith. This is a revolutionary story in which

Jesus sharply redefines the world as his disciples know it. The way things are is turned on its head as Jesus invites the woman to another understanding of the world by his words and actions. The story is set at a well associated with Jacob, where Jesus encounters a Samaritan woman. He asks for water, and the conversation moves to deeper levels about the meaning of water and the life that Jesus gives to those who see him as the face of God. The Samaritan woman recognizes who he is, and she proclaims this news to all who will hear it. Several points of particular significance are in this narrative.

First of all, Jesus' conversation with a Samaritan was out of the ordinary. Good Jews did not ordinarily associate with Samaritans, who were considered marginal to society and the established religious order. So, by calling to the woman, asking her for a drink of water, and engaging her in conversation, Jesus has already stepped over an accepted boundary. This is why the woman asks, "How is it that you, a Jew, ask a drink of me, a woman of Samaria?" (John 4:9).

Second, Jesus engages the woman in a conversation of the deepest theological significance. The fact that the conversation is between Jesus and a woman would not have been lost on those who first heard this story. Later when the disciples arrive at the scene, they are perplexed to see Jesus carrying on a serious conversation with a woman. Such conversations were usually the preserve of men. The text indicates they do not say anything out loud, but the writer of John lets us in on what they are thinking: "They were astonished that he was speaking with a woman, but no one said, 'What do you want?' or, 'Why are you speaking with her?'" (John 4:27).

Third, the turning point of the story comes in the woman's recognition that Jesus is carrying on a conversation at two levels. He asks for a drink of water to satisfy his thirst, but the conversation immediately moves to another level. This is not just a conversation about how to get a drink; it is a dialogue about the water of life. The woman knows this: "Sir, you have no bucket, and the well is deep. Where do you get that living water?" (John 4:11), and Jesus says, "Those who drink of the water that I will give them will never be thirsty. The water that I will give will become in them a spring of water gushing up to eternal life" (John 4:14). Then, in an act of faith, the woman finds her voice to say, "Sir, give me this water, so that I

may never be thirsty or have to keep coming here to draw water"
(John 4:15). She listens to what Jesus is saying, and she responds to his call on
her life. In hearing, she is led to believing. She is able to see what
Christ's presence means for her and how she might be changed by
this new relationship. For the first time, she understands her life.
The deepening of the moment occurs as Jesus reveals his knowledge of her. In listening to Jesus, she recognizes he knows her at the
deepest levels of her life, and out of this new understanding she
finds her voice: "Then the woman left her water jar and went back
to the city. She said to the people, 'Come and see a man who told me
everything I have ever done!'" Then it hits her and she adds: "He
cannot be the Messiah, can he?" (John 4:29). Unlike the lawyer
Nicodemus, the Samaritan woman hears and sees in Jesus a new
understanding of herself and the world.

As we hear these stories, we have to shift our own position. This
is the movement that Jesus urges upon Nicodemus and the Samaritan woman. In order to hear what Jesus is saying, we have to be
willing to suspend the assumptions we make about how the world
operates and try to see the world from another point of view. This is
our world made visible in a different way. Jesus is talking about seeing the world differently and understanding it from a different angle.
That is what the Samaritan woman does; it is what Nicodemus cannot do.

The poet William Stafford speaks of this new life:

> Time wants to show you a different country. It's the one
> that your life conceals, the one waiting outside
> when curtains are drawn, the one Grandmother hinted at
> in her crochet design, the one almost found
> over at the edge of the music, after the sermon.[3]

What lies after the sermon is what we do with our lives, how we
use our time, and to what we commit our love and work. In our
search for God, we are finally pulled to some place in particular
where we may hear God speak to us and show us a "different country." Instead of trying to question God, we find ourselves addressed

by God with questions that change our lives and move us in a new direction. This is the critical point of change, that is, an unwillingness to keep going with the way things are and a willingness to accept God's call on our lives. The kind of learning that forms the practices of the Christian life occurs in a community of faith where our usual ways of thinking are turned around by the gospel's angle of vision.

In congregations this means taking time to listen to one another, to practice forms of hospitality within and beyond the church's walls which invite the kind of sharing and inquiry that can help us form the questions we need to address. If we lose patience and jump too quickly to the problem-solving mode, then we are probably going to diminish the complexity of the issues we face and render superficial the questions we raise. Most of all, this kind of patience requires faith that trusts God to speak in the midst of our common life. In such a spirit we may find new energy and imagination.[4]

SIX

~

Wisdom and Folly

Has not God made foolish the wisdom of the world? For since, in the wisdom of God, the world did not know God through wisdom, God decided, through the foolishness of our proclamation, to save those who believe.

—1 Corinthians 1:20–21

The kingdom of God comes not through logical concepts but through surprises.

—Christoph Friedrich Blumhardt[1]

THE TRUTH OF THE GOSPEL—the story of Jesus' life, death, and resurrection—is not a matter of abstract knowledge. We know and are known, as Paul said, only as we are able to love (1 Cor. 13). This way of knowing involves suffering, passion, and joy. It is not neutral. While the usual symbol of intellectual excellence is the golden mean that balances out everything, makes it neat and clean, the symbol of learning in the Christian tradition is a piece of wood in the shape of a cross. Most often this learning comes in the form of stories, and the most important stories are told by those we love and admire.

Growing up, I remember overhearing the stories of adults. Listening to those conversations, I heard stories told and retold, and without being instructed, I had a hunch that language was an invention that called for continuing creation. No one had to tell me what was literally true, because I knew that stories pointed to truth and led me into mystery. The church has to recover this kind of storytelling if faith is to be passed from generation to generation. Our hope for the recovery of this tradition lies in the recognition that stories lead us into the fullness of our lives, and we cannot live without them.[2]

Old stories are transformed by new moments. New stories are told as we retell and interpret the events of our lives. In this sense, stories move us forward at the same time that they take us back to another time. They give us courage, they lead us toward faith, and in them we find wisdom.

One of the best stories I know is the familiar story of Ruby Bridges and Robert Coles. In 1960, when she was six years old, Ruby Bridges became the first African American child to attend the William Frantz Elementary School in New Orleans. Each day over several months she walked with federal marshals through an angry crowd protesting her presence. Ruby's story has often been told by the Harvard psychiatrist Robert Coles, who was an air force medical officer in the area when he learned of Ruby's ordeal. He thought that observing her behavior during this struggle could help him learn something about children in crisis.[3]

As Coles received permission for this research and became acquainted with Ruby, he watched for signs of distress. When he asked her how she was doing, though, she simply replied, "Fine." She indicated that her appetite was good, she was able to sleep at night, and except for the difficulty of her daily walk through the mob, her life continued in its usual pattern. One day, however, Ruby's teacher mentioned to Coles that she had noticed that Ruby seemed to be talking to herself as she made her way to school. Coles seized upon this as the visible sign of dysfunction that he had expected. He asked Ruby if it was true: Did she talk to herself? Ruby responded that she did not talk to herself or to the crowd; rather, she was talking to God. She prayed to God before and after school each day as she walked through the mob:

> Please, God, try to forgive those people.
> Because even if they say those bad things,
> They don't know what they're doing.
> So You could forgive them,
> Just like You did those folks a long time ago
> When they said terrible things about You.[4]

Ruby continued her walk to school, the Frantz Elementary School was integrated, and she completed her education. Robert Coles has called six-year-old Ruby Bridges his most important teacher. He admits he learned more from her about courage and faith than from anyone else in his own education. Coles could not at first understand how this child could act in such an extraordinary way, with seemingly no recognition that it was out of the ordinary at all. She did what she felt she had to do. She acted out of beliefs and values that she learned in her family and church. Coles tells us that one day when he was questioning Ruby in the attempt to get at her motivations, Ruby's mother finally intervened to point out the obvious: Ruby could not be understood by herself; she belonged to a community, a tradition, that had ways of knowing what was right and what was wrong. This community, most of all her family and church, lived within a tradition that provided her with ways of seeing the world and ways of acting so deeply ingrained that they were "habits of being."[5] The congregation in which she was raised had stories to tell of how men and women had acted faithfully out of beliefs that gave meaning to the world and direction to how we are to live: to love our neighbors, to forgive our enemies, and to give thanks to God. This is the church's best wisdom, a way of belonging that is an encounter with truth and love.[6]

The story of Ruby Bridges is most of all the account of Robert Coles's recognition that something was present in her life that could not be explained away by any system of analysis. In a poem, Dr. Coles describes the turning in his life that was brought about by the presence of Ruby Bridges:

> One question a kindly doctor
> Sitting way out of sight
> But working to hear
> Answered by not answering:
> "I don't know what to say,"
> Thereby giving permission
> To find out what *you* had to say,
> A job that became a rescue,
> Mine by you,

> Though, it did take you time:
> The "resistance" we doctors
> Are heard to mention—
> Always when talking of others.[7]

Six-year-old Ruby Bridges raised a question in Coles's mind and heart that could not be answered easily by any of the standard responses he had learned in his formal education. Ruby Bridges turned Robert Coles's life around and converted him to another way of seeing and being in the world.

For me this story raises an essential issue for a weary church: What difference does it make for children to be raised in a Christian community of faith? Is there anything distinctive about their education that forms their outlooks and actions in the same way the New Orleans congregation did for Ruby? How does the gospel get taught as a way of helping us deal with the public and private, the hidden and unseen ways we live in the world? Most of what passes as Christian education is a kind of ideal version of the good life framed in a middle-class culture. Much of the time, children and young people take all this in, listen obediently, then put this religious instruction behind them as something that pertains to church but has almost nothing to do with making their way through recess, dealing with the achievements and disappointments of school, or facing the power and relationship struggles that emerge even in the sandbox. Charles Lemert writes, "Social things come down upon us, and we, if we will, take them into ourselves, thus to carry forth the world in our small corners. The world is perfectly able to crush the human spirit. But, more often than not, the living soul takes it in, resists or weeps where possible and necessary, and fashions a life with others even if on meager wage."[8]

Ruby Bridges found courage in the kind of imagination given her by biblical narratives that told her about prophets and apostles, courageous women and faithful men, who had faced oppression and experienced suffering. In the story of Jesus she found a language of faith that showed her how to walk through that mob and permitted her to pray using words she had heard many times before. She could identify with Jesus, and she thus found in his story and continuing presence the grace to be a witness of the gospel's truth.

In light of this story, one of the places where Christian formation is most needed is with adolescents as they try to wend their way through the maze of high school life. Young people are taught in high school that the best are always the brightest and the most talented. High scores on aptitude tests, acceptance in key social groups, and participation in academic tracks leading to college admission make up the triad that determines how young people will be valued in our culture. There is a special niche reserved for star athletes, but many of their dreams fade as the realities of collegiate and professional sports come into view. Nowhere in the midst of this socialization process is there any reflection about what purposes we are called to serve or what work we will do. Almost all of the actual jobs expressing a sense of purpose or calling are regarded as low status work. As a society, we focus inordinately on children and youth, yet we pay inadequate salaries to the teachers and counselors who work with them. The teacher, who helps young persons find a way of overcoming difficult circumstances, receives a pittance of recognition for this work. At the same time, the attorney, who might defend the same youths if they got into trouble, receives a relatively large financial reward for that service. We see these contradictions, but we do nothing about them because of our captivity to "the way things are."

Ruby Bridges learned the practices of faith in a Christian community where "the way things are" was questioned in light of "the way things should be." Her family had few of the resources that protect most of us from the worst inroads of the world on our lives, yet her family members were able to respond when the destructive power of society threatened to overwhelm them. They belonged to a church that helped them live with faith and courage. Isn't this the kind of church we yearn to be?

SEVEN

~

A New Belonging

Now you are the body of Christ and individually members of it.

—1 Corinthians 12:27

Learning is first a new belonging.

—Kurt Lewin[1]

WITHIN THE CHRISTIAN COMMUNITY, learning is, first of all, a new belonging; it is truth known in relationship. In the biblical narratives, the issue of belonging is a continuing question. It is the question of origins, purpose and, ultimately, the place from which we will view the world. What we know, whom we love, and the nature of our learning all depend upon our sense of relationship. The image of learning taking place in an isolated individual is a naive fantasy. Even in silence and solitude, we stand before another who calls us in the depths of our being. In *The Heidelberg Catechism*, the first question is, "What is your only comfort, in life and in death?" The answer given is, "That I belong—body and soul, in life and in death—not to myself but to my faithful Saviour, Jesus Christ." Not "I believe" or "I think," but "I belong."[2]

My first recognition that there was some connection between the gospel and a community of faith occurred when I was a child. The setting was the Sunday school assembly of the congregation to which my family had belonged for many years. We lived in another town, but we had come back to visit relatives in the small eastern Kentucky railroad town that had once been home. I remember hearing the Sunday school superintendent call the gathering to order and invite someone to pray. I looked around to see who it would be, and then I heard my grandfather's voice. I had heard him pray before as he said grace at home, but I had not heard him pray in public. It was a new thing for me to see an inward path so publicly expressed. Most important, it led me to see that in the assembly there was a community to which I belonged and a truth from which I could learn and shape my life. None of this was self-evident at the time, but over the years that early recognition of belonging was the tentative first step in the way that has most formed my life. Learning that evokes such a sense of communion calls to us at the most significant levels of our lives. This is a way of knowing that claims us; it is truth that saves us. Part of the problem we face in understanding this kind of learning is the captivity of all education to mercantilistic language. We have so defined education as a mode of production that even our metaphors are shaped by financial ends. For example, our usual argument on behalf of schooling is based on the claim of how much money an education will produce for an individual. We make further claims that education enables one to manage life better, provides skills, techniques, and means of problem solving that give us control and access to power. The difficulty, as the novelist Walker Percy once pointed out, is that we may "make all A's and flunk life."[3]

Embedded within this economic and managerial mode of education is the assumption that learning itself is a transfer of information: the teacher is there to give it, and the student is there to receive it. There is little sense of dialogue or relationship in such a view of education. Furthermore, the individualistic nature of our culture makes it almost impossible for us to sustain communities in which we may belong to one another and to traditions that provide meaning and significance for our lives. While we have many organizations, we have few communities. What we call community is often simply an enclave of like-minded people.

In our society, we tend to discredit the possibility of one truth being more important or more significant than another. We lean toward flattening all things, making everything equal, and in the end, we sometimes do not commit to anything that has real importance for us. The gospel points to a different way of being; it is an encounter with truth that will exercise authority in our lives. As Christians, the gospel is the story that interprets and reforms our personal narratives. It is a matter not of how this story agrees with our experience, but of how the gospel takes us to another place from which to interpret the events of our lives; it is a new experience of ourselves in the world (2 Cor. 5:17–18).

The kind of learning we are called to do and the kind of teachers we are called to be comprise a work of love; it is the only work that counts. The poet Rainer Maria Rilke once wrote that "for one human being to love another: that is perhaps the most difficult of all our tasks, the ultimate, the last test and proof, the work for which all other work is but preparation."[4] Sometimes we get the notion that we should wait until some great job comes along that will announce itself as our real work. In the meantime, we tend to devalue our lives and work. One of the most unfortunate phrases ever invented in the church was "full-time Christian service," which refers not to the way in which whatever work we do is transformed by our understanding of the gospel, but is a reference to ecclesiastical positions filled by clergy. Rilke points toward something different. It is the recognition that what ultimately matter in life are the acts of service, the ways of loving others, that define the core of our being. Most of the time this is anonymous work; it is not the kind of work that gets you on the cover of *Time*. Usually, it is work that nurtures and supports, but does not call attention to itself. Writer Tracy Kidder once suggested, "Many people find it easy to imagine unseen webs of malevolent conspiracy in the world, and they are not always wrong. But there is also an innocence that conspires to hold humanity together, and it is made of people who can never fully know the good they have done."[5]

Such persons are the fundamental forces of good in any society. They do not depend on publicity, or even on immediate acceptance of what they do, to legitimate their work; what they do is sufficient in itself. We meet these people every day, but we take for granted the power of their work to touch and transform our lives. These quiet revolutionaries, without claiming credit, engage in a struggle against the powers and principalities that often make this world a dangerous place. Such people know that religious commitment is less about finding a safe place for themselves than it is about trying as best they can to take responsibility in the places God has given them to serve. Many years ago I heard someone speak of some missioners who were serving the poorest of the poor in a part of the city seldom seen. They were asked why they were giving their lives to that service. Their response was simple and direct: "To keep alive the rumor of God."[6] The inherited symbolic construction of the Western world that guaranteed a place for God and a role for Jesus no longer exists. This shared umbrella of meaning has folded up, and what we have left is a universe without self-evident definition. The world we live in is a cynical place controlled largely by economic interests. The reduced role of religion in this kind of world is that of a chaplain in the race for power and security. It is a private place to which we may come for respite. Professional sports and mass media increasingly provide the kind of identification and entertainment once provided by religious institutions. The language of sports has created the dominant metaphors of our lives that express the basic values by which the world of popular culture is constructed.

If the church is to offer an alternative to this mass culture, it has to focus its efforts on helping us rethink the nature of belief and the substance of faith. It must offer a way of thinking that engages our minds and hearts. Most of all, it must help us find real work to do— a way of working that expresses our love of God with heart, soul, and mind. The gospel defines us primarily as persons of faith, but many people in church are there simply to feel good and to be thought good. In contrast, the gospel sees few of us as good and knows that most of the time we fall short of our best intentions.

Often we talk of faith as if it is something static, a set of propositions that are logical and unchanging. The opposite is actually true— faith is more about movement than it is about holding on. Faith, then, is about the paths we take and the turns we make. But it is especially concerned with the companions we meet on the journey and how we respond to the questions and events that occur along the way. In Hebrews, faith is defined as "the assurance of things hoped for, the conviction of things not seen" (Heb. 11:1). The text goes on to affirm, "By faith we understand that the worlds were prepared by the word of God, so that what is seen was made from things that are not visible" (Heb. 11:3). Faith is a matter of defining the world; it is about making visible the worlds that are hidden or crushed beneath the everyday life of our own local culture. This demands a suspension of our prejudgments in order to see the world as if for the first time. It is a difficult task because we live in tents of meaning that provide us with assumptions out of which we perceive the world. While it is easy to see other people's tents, it is not so easy for us to identify the shape and color of the tents we inhabit.

Throughout his life and ministry, Jesus invited men and women to step outside their tents. Faith is a continuing act of interpretation. The world is not self-evident; it requires understanding and definition. In faith we respond to the truth in which we will live. For some people, there is nothing other than the everyday world. The world for such persons is self-evident; it requires no interpretation, just endurance. In his novel *The Second Coming,* Walker Percy writes about a character: "Not once in his entire life had he allowed himself to come to rest in the quiet center of himself but had forever cast himself forward from some dark past he could not remember to a future which did not exist. Not once had he been present for his life. So his life had passed like a dream."[7]

Then Percy goes on to question, "Is it possible for people to miss their lives in the same way one misses a plane?"[8] The biblical answer to this question is *yes, we can miss our lives.* The assurance of faith is that we can find our lives only in a paradoxical way: By being willing to lose our lives, we can find them. In this sense, we are present for our lives to the extent that we are able to let go of the definitions we invent to protect us from uncertainty. In Christ, we are called beyond a mass-merchandised notion of happiness to the real joy and fulfillment that come only when they are lived out within the competing themes of suffering and pain. Left to ourselves, we find the work of love an impossible task, yet by God's grace such work can become our work as the people of God. In relearning the gospel, in hearing again the radical word of Jesus Christ, we may discover the church as the community that preaches, nurtures, and expresses this vocation as its fundamental reason for being. In such a discovery, we may be freed from the stranglehold of institutional anxiety long enough to envision the congregation as Christ's missionary community. Congregational life becomes the setting in which we learn and form the practices of faith that guide our work and the service we embody in response to God's calling.

EIGHT

~

Vocation
The Hope of Our Calling

There is one body and one Spirit, just as you were called to the one hope of your calling.

—Ephesians 4:4

The primary Christian vocation is to accomplish responsibly our human vocation: to be partners of God in the ongoing work of creation.

—Hans-Ruedi Weber, *Living in the Image of Christ*[1]

THE CHRISTIAN VOCATION is shaped by God who calls us to love and to work; it is the common witness of those who follow Jesus Christ. This summons is the fundamental calling given to all of us in baptism. Vocation is our calling by God in the diverse moments, situations, and issues of our lives. It is the experience of hearing God calling us by name and summoning us to a new perspective, a particular responsibility, and a larger vision. This calling speaks within us, but it is focused in ministry, mission, and service. For Christians, this event is, most of all, mediated and interpreted by Christ's presence. It involves the reinterpretation of our lives in light of Christ's call to turn around, confess, and witness to the goodness and mercy of God. This experience may occur in an unpredictable moment, or it may emerge after many moments that together form a pattern in which we discern a calling. Vocation, however, is not a single, unchanging sense of purpose. Throughout our lives, we live in the midst of several callings, changing times, and new understandings of God's voice. Our calling as persons shaped by the claims of God is a meandering journey; it is not a straight path. God leads us in purposeful, yet subtle, ways that give meaning to our lives and our work and, in effect, give us new life and new work.

God does not require us to know exactly where we are going. Faithfulness requires a certain flexibility that permits us to change course as the wind blows and shifts direction and we are called to places of suffering and deep joy. God asks us to be ready for those moments, to reach out and to move with the Spirit to unexpected places, for "the wind blows where it chooses" (John 3:8). In the water of baptism, we are called by name and drawn onward to the ministry of Christ. The work of ministry begins in the recognition of the essential calling of all Christians; it marks the church's giving of its own life to the world.

In a broader sense, our calling as Christians makes us aware that to speak of vocation is to talk about what it means to be human, the purposes for which we live, and the ends toward which we move. This is the fundamental promise of each child newborn to the world. "In every child who is born, under no matter what circumstances, and of no matter what parents, the potentiality of the human race is born again."[2] As James Agee goes on to indicate, the birth of a child claims every one of us who will share in his or her life. In a child's birth, we are recalled to "our terrific responsibility towards human life; towards the utmost idea of goodness, of the horror of error, and of God."[3]

From cradle to grave, in different periods of life as youths or adults, parents or children, friends or lovers, we embody a variety of roles and responsibilities, and we must live through different situations and circumstances. By and large, others see us partially, that is, as what we represent to them. But what calls us forth is what names us, what we are that no one else is. As fleeting as this moment may be, it is there as memory to which we may return, and it is there as hope, the forward motion of our lives. In *Markings*, Dag Hammarskjöld affirms: "I don't know Who—or what—put the question, I don't know when it was put. I don't even remember answering. But at some moment I did answer 'Yes' to Someone—or Something—and from that hour I was certain that existence is meaningful and that, therefore, my life, in self-surrender, had a goal."[4]

On another level, vocation often takes the form of a question in our lives. Each of us wrestles with particular questions that are shaped by our experience. What we need, though, are radical questions that go to the heart of the matter: "Where do we come from? Who are we? Where are we going?"[5] These are questions about the mysteries of time, the discrepancies of wealth and poverty, and the dynamics of power and powerlessness that frame the pain, suffering, and hope of the world. Within the community of faith, we recognize that these are questions of God, who forms the questions in our hearts and calls us to respond. Eugen Rosenstock-Huessy once said, "[God] is the power which makes us speak . . . [who] puts words of life on our lips."[6] A woman who is unschooled, yet wise in her understanding of vocation, recounts, "My Momma told me: remember that you're put here only for a few seconds of God's time, and He's testing you. He doesn't want answers, though. He wants you to know how to ask the right questions."[7]

Too often we search for answers, settle for what is available, and then hide behind them for the rest of our days. Although doing this may promote security, ultimately it is boring, bland, and essentially irresponsible. In the effort to protect our answers, our lives become ready-made puzzles with precut pieces. Accordingly, to speak of vocation is to look at the various pieces that go into the making of our lives and to see the pattern that shapes these particularities.

We should examine our sense of vocation in moments of centering, as well as in moments of disequilibrium, when we feel torn apart. Usually in looking back and piecing many different moments together, we begin to realize there is a pattern. The novelist Eudora Welty writes, "The events in our lives happen in a sequence in time, but in their significance to ourselves they find their own order, a timetable not necessarily—perhaps not possibly—chronological. That time as we know it subjectively is often the chronology that stories and novels follow: it is the continuous thread of revelation."[8]

In this regard, Mary Catherine Bateson speaks "about life as an improvisatory art, about the ways we combine familiar and unfamiliar components in response to new situations, following an underlying grammar and an evolving aesthetic."[9] She illuminates and deepens the question of vocation by helping us understand that the fact of change itself implies something that is ongoing: "Change proposes constancy: What is the ongoing entity of which we can say that it has assumed a new form? A composite life poses the recurring riddle of what the parts have in common."[10] The "ongoing entity," the spirit that takes different forms, is the vision out of which our lives take shape; it is a story told in diverse moments with a changing set of characters; it is a task that is never finished because new moments create new meanings. Yet among the changing colors and patterns of our lives, there is "the thread that runs so true."[11]

In the Christian life, vocation is not a matter of self-actualization in some popular psychological sense; it is how we may hear a voice that calls each of us by name (Isa. 43:1). It is not simply that we see what has always been present, though that is a significant part of our understanding; rather, something new comes into view as we hear God's call. What we have always known is no longer quite the same. Our self-definitions, convictions, and assumptions are transformed as we view them from a new vantage point. While we must remain open and searching, ultimately we are called by something outside ourselves that is not dependent on our will.

This something is Someone, Jesus Christ, who does for us what we cannot do by ourselves. We might want to cross the borders of our lives, yet more often than not we cannot carry through, and the new self we projected ourselves becoming ends up as the same old self we thought we had left behind. As Dietrich Bonhoeffer points out, it is precisely at this boundary where Christ stands for us. He stands "between me and myself, between the old 'I' and the new 'I.'"[12] "At this place," he writes, "I cannot stand alone. Here Christ stands, in the centre, between me and myself, between the old existence and the new. So Christ is at the same time my own boundary and my rediscovered centre."[13]

Vocation, then, is actually more a matter of being found than finding. It is more the experience of being sought than searching. The voice that calls us is the God who comes to us from a place beyond our own imagination. We are forever changed when we hear this call to follow a different way, to set out in a different direction, and to see the world from a new vantage point (2 Cor. 5:16–17).

The Appalachian preacher in James Still's *River of Earth* speaks of the change in his understanding of the horizon out of which he lived. "I was borned in a ridge-pocket," the preacher says, "... I never seed the sun-ball without heisten my chin. My eyes were sot upon the hills from the beginning. Till I come on the Word in this good Book, I used to think a mountain was the standingest object in the sight o' God." But then in the new light of Christ, he realizes that "these hills are jist dirt waves, washing through eternity." The question, of course, emerging from this revised perspective is the primary issue of vocation: "Oh, my children, where air we going on this mighty river of earth, a-borning, begetting, and a-dying—the living and the dead riding the waters? What air it sweeping us?"[14]

Vocation is the sense of our lives as a gift and of life as a mystery whose purpose is revealed in diverse ways to each of us, though never fully comprehended. Although vocation has come to refer to our occupations, vocation essentially is about who we are and what we are called to become. It is not a matter of wanting to be a doctor, a lawyer, or a chief of anything. For too long we have discussed the nature of vocation in a way that applies only to the professions. God calls us at far more significant levels of meaning than can be identified with certain roles in society. There are no occupations that in themselves are sanctified expressions of calling. The end toward which any work is directed determines whether or not it is a form of love and a means of service. We know, in this sense, that the physician may practice medicine, but not be concerned with healing; the attorney may argue cases, but not pursue justice; and the pastor may preach without believing anything at all. In the biblical tradition it is more often than not the dispossessed, those without jobs, the despised and rejected of society, who are instruments of God's purposes in the world. Our work may express our vocation, but it does not contain it.[15]

In thinking about the nature of vocation, we begin with the calling of the people of God. It is within this corporate calling that an individual is called by name. One of the most eloquent expressions of that calling is in Isaiah:

> But now thus says God,
> the One who created you, O Jacob,
> the One who formed you, O Israel:
> Do not fear, for I have redeemed you;
> I have called you by name, you are mine. (43:1)

These words, and their power, are etched into the memory of Israel. This larger sense of a people's calling provides a context for understanding vocation as it is expressed in an individual person.[16] Vocation involves the direction of our lives in this moment, for all time, and even before time. Remember the words of Jeremiah:

> Now the word of God came to me saying,
> "Before I formed you in the womb I knew you,
> and before you were born I consecrated you;
> I appointed you a prophet to the nations." (1:4–5)

The first word Jeremiah says in response to God's call is, "Ah, Sovereign God! Truly I do not know how to speak, for I am only a boy." God replies,

> Do not say, "I am only a boy";
> for you shall go to all to whom I send you,
> and you shall speak whatever I command you.
> Do not be afraid of them,
> for I am with you to deliver you. (1:6–8)

Throughout the traditions of calling, God says, "Come." Some other people such as Jonah say, "Wait just a minute! Isn't there somebody else you could call?" Or, like the persons called by Jesus, we ask for a postponement, saying, "Give me a chance to take care of a few things and then I'll consider the invitation" (Luke 9:57–62). But as the Gospel of John says, "You did not choose me but I chose you" (15:16). That character of being chosen is one of the guidelines to the authenticity and the integrity of the call. Calling is not essentially a matter of achievement. It is seldom the case that we are qualified to do what God has in mind. Most of the time those called are unlikely candidates. Think how the prophets would be measured on this issue. Vocation is not a career choice; it is the recognition of the purposes of God in our lives. That is the surprising quality of calling: it is a gift and not an entitlement. God's calling does not necessarily improve our status in society. More often than not, it does just the opposite.

Persons who are called come under what Paul Minear once termed "the law of greatness," which is simply that "the last shall be first, the most humble, the most exalted, the servant of all the greatest of all."[17] It is "the order of the towel,"[18] which is the symbol Jesus used when he washed his disciples' feet as a sign of the ministry to which he called them. Calling does not elevate us; it inclines us in a different direction and pulls us into a world that turns around all our assumptions of status.[19] With a sense of vocation, our will and our work are brought together with energy and imagination. Much of the time we live within the constraints of tension and anxiety. We intend to do one thing, yet we do something else. Sometimes, though, we mount up with wings as eagles; we run and we do not get tired; we do not fall down; we do things we could not ordinarily have done (Isa. 40:30–31). When this happens, we need to pay attention to what the moment tells us about the direction of our lives, the holy ground on which we walk, and the mystery of things we have taken for granted.

It would be simpler if the circumstances of God's call were more straightforward. If lights came on and some rendition of the "Hallelujah Chorus" played in our hearing, then we could know for sure. But that is not the way God calls us. Some persons may be able to identify a precise, particular moment when they heard God's voice. More often, though, we wend our way slowly toward the recognition of being called. "We cannot live our lives constantly looking back, listening back, lest we be turned to pillars of longing and regret," Frederick Buechner writes, "but to live without listening at all is to live deaf to the fullness of the music."[20]

Calling, then, is first of all a matter of hope; it gives us the courage to remember, and in this sense, we are called backward in order to go forward. Memory and hope work together in a mutually revealing way. Between the pull of the future and the push of the past, we are called to live in the present moment. Vocation means living in between the past and the future in the present, which is revealed by memory, hope, and promise. It concerns the fundamental reality in which we live, not some rarefied, abstracted compartment labeled "spiritual." Vocation is the recognition that God has a claim on our lives and calls us out of our own reshaped and redefined humanity in Christ to participate in the continuing transformation of this world in light of the promise of the world to come (Rev. 21:1–4).

PART THREE

Practices of Faith

~

The Presbyterian church was agreeable in winter, with its damp
cloakrooms and its snowy-haired superintendents, its subdued
hymnal and discreet baptism. More memorable and disturbing
were surreptitious visits to itinerant evangelical tent meetings.
There it was possible to be saved more than once, saved again and
again.

—Elizabeth Hardwick, *Sleepless Nights*[1]

NINE

~

The Church's Witness

You are the salt of the earth.... You are the light of the world.

—Matthew 5:13, 14

To be a witness does not mean to spread propaganda, or even to create an impression, but to *create a mystery*. It means living in such a way that one's life would be inexplicable if God did not exist.

—Cardinal Suhard, *The Pastoral Letters*[1]

IN LOOKING AT ISSUES FACING THE CHURCH, I am reminded of Flannery O'Connor's stories and her portrayal of a "country of faith" at once close by, yet strangely distant from all our preconceptions. The life that God promises and Christ reveals is more diverse than anything we might imagine. But it is nearer than we might think. As Tarwater maintains in *The Violent Bear It Away*, we need always to be aware of God's "terrible speed of mercy."[2]

Our weariness in the church exists in contrast with the boundlessness of God's grace. We are called to "run and not be weary" (Isa. 40:31), yet it is often difficult to summon such energy. To address this weariness, to find once again the faith and imagination to be Christ's church, we have to look at the nature of the church's witness in the world. This world in which we live is a kind of marketplace where everything has a price; nothing is exempt from the threat of becoming a commodity. Ideas as well as pork bellies are up for trade and speculation. We market ideas as much as we develop new products. Our lives are measured by what we have to sell and how much we can buy; nothing has value in itself. In this context, our relationships with one another are primarily instrumental because there is no inherent sense of mutuality; the only real measure of relationship is often one of contract and obligation.[3]

In this world as marketplace, meaning is found through seeking out others who share our views. There is no public truth that has claim over other claims, for everything is up for barter and trade. We are left to our own devices and desires to construct some personal meaning that will give us a sense of purpose. However, this search is never-ending. What meaning we find one day often disappears the next because we no longer feel its significance for us.

In an effort to sustain some kind of stable state, we construct private associations that give us a semblance of order and purpose even though those purposes and that order may change quickly. Admission to these various gatherings depends on shared meanings and social background. They are stratified on the basis of income, race, social class, and education. If we have the right credentials, then we can become part of a group that provides some support amid the wear and tear of our everyday lives. These associations are varied and diverse. They range from elite professional associations to political interest groups. They are ethnic clubs, neighborhood associations, racial caucuses, and Internet talk groups. The church has also become such a group.

The church provides a meeting place, a group of friends, and a way of periodically expressing some form of service to the community's needs. The church is all the more appealing as a private place of meaning because its sacred canopy can provide a sense of superiority over other associations. In the various aspects of its life, though, the church functions essentially like other associations.

In contrast with this usual way of being, the church is not just a social institution; it is Christ's body. That calling should distinguish it from other voluntary associations. The church is not just a human creation, for God determined its origin and end. This vocation expresses its redeemed and broken character and requires the church to be a community whose reformation continues without end. The fact is the church is in the world; the question is how the church's vocation as the body of Christ informs its presence, shapes its purposes, and equips its members for ministry.[4]

Many of our notions of church and world have been shaped by the medieval imagery of enclosures and walls. As castles were designed to keep out enemies, so were monasteries constructed as independent communities whose gates would shut out the influence of the so-called secular world. In this mentality, the world was outside the gate. Men and women left secular society to enter the sacred community. What is clear, though, is eventually how dependent the monastery was on the secular world to sustain its life. It took an enormous amount of peasant labor in the monastery fields to support the monks in their life of prayer. A form of sacred barter was created in which the monks received their daily bread from those outside the monastery's enclosure and in turn prayed for the laborers and for other benefactors.

Sometimes we speak of the church as if it is removed from the world rather than a distinctive presence in the world. However, there is no place we can go that is not the world. The true role of the church is to teach an understanding of the nature of the world and our place in it, which is based on the reality of God as the radical other in the midst of all we take for granted. In Jesus Christ, God calls us to something other than the values and perceptions that have shaped our usual view of things. John Calvin suggested that coming to faith was like putting on a pair of glasses through which, for the first time, we actually begin to see the world with some clarity.[5] The difficulty is that we think we see fine, and even if we wear some kind of eyeglasses, we assume the prescription is correct. To take off the old and put on the new lens is an invitation to faith; it is to see the church beyond the enclosure, *in* the world as a radically different presence.

The church called into being by God puts us in the world without any assumptions of entitlement or exemption from the human condition. There should be no pretense in this community of faith that we are somehow removed from the brokenness that characterizes the whole world. Our calling as God's people is to become a community that lives in, often over against, but always for the world despite its brokenness. The tension created between the versions of the world in which we live and Christ's revised version of the world is the creative tension in which we are called to ministry. When this tension is released by the church, it becomes one more private association.

In a society that increasingly is divided into enclaves of the like-minded, the church's witness is to be a community of diversity. Inclusiveness is not an option up for vote in the church. We distort the biblical call to build up the body of Christ when we view diversity as something to consider *after* we have taken care of other issues. On the other hand, inclusiveness is not the product of a divine quota system. Diversity is the gift of the Spirit, and an inclusive church is formed by the power of its witness to the gospel, which calls us to the borders of difference and the edges of predictability where Christ can break through the "fences of our nature."[6]

The diversity of the church is found not in the sum total of its members, not in any definition of inclusiveness that we create, but in the presence of Christ, who is the center of the community of faith.[7] Out of our relationship to such singularity, we can celebrate and embrace the genuine diversity in which we live:

> For he is our peace; in his flesh he has made both groups into one and has broken down the dividing wall, that is, the hostility between us. He has abolished the law with its commandments and ordinances, that he might create in himself one new humanity in place of the two, thus making peace, and might reconcile both groups to God in one body through the cross, thus putting to death that hostility through it. (Eph. 2:14–16)

This picture of the reconciled community of Jesus Christ is obviously different from most mainline congregations that are essentially homogeneous in their members' cultural and racial backgrounds. The promise of a new humanity summons us together, but we seldom experience this social reality in our congregations. The hope of this passage from Ephesians is that a diverse and even fundamentally hostile group of people can be united by their faith in Jesus Christ, whose presence effects the reconciliation.

A congregation that celebrates genuine diversity does so in the confidence of its faith in a God who allows us to understand one another even though we may not be able to speak one another's language. This is the testimony of Pentecost:

> Parthians, Medes, Elamites, and residents of Mesopotamia, Judea and Cappadocia, Pontus and Asia, Phrygia and Pamphylia, Egypt and the parts of Libya belonging to Cyrene, and visitors from Rome, both Jews and proselytes, Cretans and Arabs—in our own languages we hear them speaking about God's deeds of power. (Acts 2:9-11)

All our plans and expectations for an inclusive church fall away if they are not centered first of all in the promise of the gospel, which informs us that such diversity is not our achievement. The ministry of reconciliation is not a communitarian experiment; it is the act of God in Jesus Christ. Without this understanding, our efforts to build the kind of church we envision always fall short. We become exhausted by the effort and demoralized by our countless failures if our hopes are not grounded in commitment to the revelation of God in Jesus Christ—the One who has broken down the wall of hostility.[8]

The foundation of an inclusive church is evangelism: the church's witness to the gospel. As a missionary structure, the church is called to tell the story of Jesus and to share this tradition of faith. The teaching ministry of the church is central as we proclaim, interpret, and seek to understand the meaning of the gospel for our lives. This evangelical task calls us to be formed in the gospel so that we are credible witnesses to the truth we preach; it is the never-ending commitment to being Christian in our lives and work. Basic to this ministry is the need to invite others to hear the truth of the gospel and to be formed in this way. The church that is built on its faith and knowledge of Jesus Christ is a church that invites, nurtures, and encourages others to share in this good news.

TEN

~

The Church's Worship

I hate, I despise your festivals,
and I take no delight in your solemn assemblies.

—Amos 5:21

And does the popularity of a religion that employs the full
resources of vaudeville drive more traditional conceptions into
manic and trivial displays? . . . I know of one rabbi who has
seriously proposed to his congregation that Luciano Pavarotti be
engaged to sing Kol Nidre at a Yom Kippur service. He believes
that the event would fill the synagogue as never before. Who can
doubt it? But as Hannah Arendt would say, *that* is the problem, not
a solution to one.

—Neil Postman, *Amusing Ourselves to Death*[1]

A T THE CENTER OF CONGREGATIONAL life is worship. Living in a
culture of entertainment, though, the church falls too easily
into the amusement trap; it becomes a sideshow where we "amuse
ourselves to death." Worship turns into another talk show, punctu-
ated by a variety of inspirational acts. Not long ago, I heard a pastor
assert that his congregation liked to refer to its service of worship as
the "Happy Hour." What happens when the worship of God is refer-
enced in such terms? As C. S. Lewis maintained in *The Screwtape
Letters*, the devil does not have to undermine the church; the church
does very well at undermining itself.[2] For example, notice how fre-
quently in our descriptions of events in the life of the church we
talk about "having an experience." In church bulletins, persons attending worship are sometimes urged to have "a good worship experience," which suggests a lack of the sense of being invited by God

to be part of a reality that is there before us and will remain after us. In this context, worship is not so much doxology as it is entertainment.

An obvious expression of the theological disarray in worship can be seen in clergy vestments, which are often worn with little understanding of the traditions they represent. Observing a distinguished cleric once, I estimated that the various symbols he wore represented at least five hundred years of conflict in church history—all on one chest. When I have asked clergy about the various items worn, I have heard them explain that they chose this robe, that alb, those colors, these stoles because they liked the way they looked. The idea that the colors, vestments, and crosses represent theological commitments does not seem to be a consideration. Of course, if worship is seen as religious entertainment, then the vestments are indeed nothing more than matters of individual taste. However, if worship is the worship of God and the gathering of the church around mission, then something so visible as the clothing worn by the persons leading worship signals what is understood as the nature of the event. Both the plain style of Quakers and the sacramental robes of Episcopalians are liturgical vestments. They express distinctive definitions of the church.[3]

The current state of worship in the church reflects distress in the community of Jesus Christ. We have borrowed liturgical practices from one another in an uncritical way that renders them insubstantive, merely decorative. But the greater distress is found in the tonality of worship that appears similarly in all denominations—a tone formed by mass culture that robs worship of its transcendent reference, substitutes coziness for mystery, and trivializes the gospel. Captive to privatized notions of God, we turn to Christ as a friendly therapist who meets us for an hour of wholesome entertainment on Sunday mornings. The preacher is a casual chaplain who has a few good stories that confirm what we have already read in the self-help columns or on the sports pages of the daily newspaper.

One reason some local congregations tilt worship toward entertainment is the fear that unless new techniques and modern devices are appropriated, sparsely attended services will become even emptier. This survivalist mode makes us do silly things and lose confidence in the only thing that counts, namely, the question of whether our worship of God is a genuine act of thanksgiving and a form of service in behalf of the church's mission in the world.

At the present time, many churches are so desperate for members that they have turned into three-ring circuses, which will import any sideshow promising a modicum of success. Ironically, just as the church is creating three rings in its circuslike activities, a new circus is appearing that reclaims an older tradition. These smaller circuses, which use only one ring, invite audiences to participate in mystery rather than be entertained by the pyrotechnics of daredevil acts. Moreover, many of these new circuses are given a narrative framework by a character, often a clown, who is a kind of teacher and storyteller.[4]

It is curious that as the church convinces itself that it has to do anything and everything to meet the needs and expectations of so-called modern life, these new circuses appropriate traditions that the church ought to know something about. While some congregations get rid of anything that suggests mystery, the new circuses understand themselves to be places of awe and wonder. As crosses, hymn books, and traditional elements of church space are removed from the congregation's place of worship in order to make visitors feel at home, we actually remove the heart of liturgy, which is composed of language and symbol that have to be learned and not simply translated into the most colloquial speech.

In describing the new circuses, Ernest Albrecht indicates identifiable elements: a sense of style, drama, distinctive music, and a feeling of family and unity. Each act is carefully planned and executed. There is attention to beauty, but no effort to trick. Circus members perform so close to the audience that an intimacy is established that is seldom matched in other forms of drama. The new circus is a significant renewal of a traditional form and the gathering of a community committed to this distinctive project. The new circuses have accomplished this renewal by the development of an artistic vision, a dedication to quality and hard work, and an appreciation that at the heart of the circus is mystery, not chicanery.[5]

In the effort to attract new members, congregations move without thinking to the Ringling Brothers, Barnum & Bailey three-ring circus model. Whether it is the possibility of Pavarotti leading a Yom Kippur service at the local Jewish synagogue, or throwing out the choir in order to bring in the chorus line, orchestra, and overhead projections, we need to stop and consider what we are doing. As I have tried to suggest, new options have appeared in the circus world that bring back an older form of the circus, which is at the same time a contemporary expression of what the circus at its best tries to represent, namely, a place of mystery. In particular, this smaller, more defined circus suggests that simplicity can provide larger meanings than the frenetic attempt to meet every need, program every minute, and fill up every silence. We need to find once again our liturgical vision with which to define worship. We cannot do this if we are primarily concerned about what will please the greatest number of people. There can be no renewal of worship without a sense of calling—a reclaiming of our distinctive vocation to be Christ's body in a particular place—which permits us to partake of the excellence and beauty of God.[6]

To think again about the worship of the church is to reconsider how the congregation comes together in thanksgiving to hear the gospel and gain some clarity about the calling of God in our lives. The liturgy emerges from the traditions that have called the congregation into being; it is "local speech" in a specific place that knows that it is part of a wider world.[7]

Liturgy, however, is not captive to the present moment. While expressive of the vernacular, it is also a word that points to the transcendent, to God's word that claims and redeems us. T. S. Eliot once spoke of poetry in language that describes the nature of liturgy as well: "So in poetry [read liturgy] you can, now and then, penetrate into another country, so to speak, before your passport has been issued or your ticket taken."[8]

Often when we think of renewing worship, we assume that this means imitating more formal or liturgical churches. Usually this spells disaster, as congregations import elements of other traditions that do not fit with their theology or practices. Becoming more liturgical simply means paying attention to the theological tradition of the congregation and thinking about what it means to make this tradition contemporary in practice. The way a Baptist church answers this question should be very different from the response of a Lutheran church down the street. Most of all, the renewal of worship emerges from the church's recognition that it is a living tradition called to practice its faith in the issues that call it to service. By way of example, a local United Church of Christ congregation in Melrose, Massachusetts,[9] woke up one day to find that some vandals had sprayed anti-Semitic and hate-filled epithets on the doors of the church. Instead of having the custodian remove the offending words and signs before the church met on Sunday, church leaders dealt with the situation as a liturgical moment, literally *leitourgia*, "the work of the people."

On the Sunday following the incident, the congregation focused on the desecration of the church doors and the evil the act represented. As part of the morning service, the congregation gathered on the steps of the church. Scraps of sandpaper were passed out among the congregation. One by one, members of the church stepped forward to remove the offending words and signs. The baptismal water from an earlier part of the service was used to wash clean the doors. The words of the litany were shaped around remembrance of the Holocaust and Christ's call to reconciliation.

Although we use words of our own making in worship, occasionally they are transposed by God's presence, and we are given a vision of another way of being in the world, of time fulfilled, of life and work filled with the power and holiness of God. When a local congregation reclaims the connection between worship and mission, it renews its life.

ELEVEN

~

Stewards

Think of us in this way, as servants of Christ and stewards of God's mysteries.

—1 Corinthians 4:1

An ethical life is one that is mindful, mannerly, and has style.

—Gary Snyder, *The Practice of the Wild*[1]

O UR CALLING BY GOD in the work of hands, heart, and mind is expressed in the way we draw relationships between faith and money, time and talent, our expectations and the needs of the world. A congregation comes to life as it recognizes that the gospel is not its possession and the church is not something it owns; instead, both gospel and church are entrusted to us by God—we are stewards whose ministry is the service we do, the work that is transformed by God's presence and purpose in the world.

An important learning about the nature of stewardship was given to me by a person I met on a trip to California while serving Eden Seminary. Every year for a number of years, Michael Lewis had contributed to the school's annual fund, and his contribution had been matched by the corporation for which he worked.[2]

The information on Mr. Lewis was somewhat sketchy. We knew he worked for a major aeronautical firm outside Los Angeles, but no one was aware of his position or much else about his life. I wanted to get acquainted with him and thank him for his commitment to the school. When I contacted him before the trip, I reached him at home and was able to set up a lunch meeting. We agreed to meet in the lobby of the corporate headquarters.

On the scheduled day, I arrived a bit early for the appointment and had some time to get a sense of the activities in the large lobby.

There was the usual reception desk, various people were coming and going, and a few maintenance workers were repairing an electrical unit. When the time for the appointment had come and gone, I asked the receptionist if she had seen Michael Lewis and indicated that I was scheduled to meet him. The receptionist was friendly and said that she had just seen him in the lobby, but he obviously had gone somewhere else. I waited another ten minutes, and then the receptionist beckoned to me and said, "Mike's just over there." While I glanced at a few executive types getting off the elevator, she pointed to the maintenance workers and indicated that he was the one wearing an orange cap.

I went over to Mr. Lewis and introduced myself. He asked me to call him Mike and apologized for getting caught up in his work, but said he would be finished in a few minutes and then we could find a place for lunch. When Mike completed his task, we went out to the parking lot, got into his car, and headed down the road. Since he wanted to show me the sights, we drove around the plant and then took a detour by his house and neighborhood. During the hour or so of the tour, I learned that Mike had grown up on a farm in Pennsylvania. He was an only child raised in a family closely related to the church. When I asked him why he had supported the seminary all those years, he indicated that his parents had told him since he was a child that he had a responsibility to support the mission of the church. He had chosen the seminary because he had been close to a pastor who had been one of its graduates. He wanted to support the school that had educated someone who had influenced his life and served the church. "My parents," Mike affirmed, "simply told me that giving was part of what you did as a grown-up."

As I thanked Mike for his support, he reiterated that giving was simply part of his life—something so taken for granted that he was surprised anyone noticed. Well, we did notice, and Mike's story has been a reminder to me of the limited way in which we think about stewardship, and the blinders we wear in thinking about those who support institutions at fundamental levels of commitment. I had assumed that Mr. Michael Lewis was a corporate executive in a business suit, wing tips, and all the other appointments of the privileged. When Michael Lewis, corporate executive, turned out to be

Mike Lewis, maintenance worker, my assumptions were revealed as the same kind of arrogance that defines so much of what and whom we think important. Mike's gift was not exactly the widow's mite, but it was close to it. Here was a significant commitment given in genuine humility out of a fundamental sense of responsibility. I have never forgotten that appointment at noon or the conversation with Mike Lewis on the practice of stewardship.

At the center of the issue of stewardship is the relationship between faith and money. The church's current fiscal picture is framed by data that show how the percentage of family income given to institutions has declined from 3.1 percent in the 1960s to 2.5 percent in the 1990s for an annual decrease of $2.8 billion.[3] This is a structural problem that sets much of the context of U.S. church life and makes stewardship central to our thinking about the purpose and mission of the church.

As we recognize the financial issues facing the church, we sometimes assume that the best way to attract new members is to develop as many programs as possible to meet the needs of its members and attract new ones as well. Robert Wuthnow, the Princeton sociologist of religion, has raised questions concerning this program orientation of many congregations. Wuthnow pursues this question: How does the program-driven church go beyond making "everyone feel at home" to fulfill "an obligation to challenge those who come to lead better lives than they would otherwise?"[4] Moreover, given the pressure of work schedules, multiple commitments, and dual-career marriages in many middle-class families, he suggests that people do not need more programs and activities; they need deeper experiences in which they can discern the gospel as another way of looking at their lives, and the church as a different kind of experience in the world.[5] The fiscal implications of this shift are that as long as the church is perceived essentially as another middle-class leisure activity, it competes with other similar programs that ask for financial and personal involvement. The likelihood is that the fiscal strength of the church will increase only as it deepens its identity as a community of faith and nurture.[6] The reality of spiritual things in connection with the social facts and demands of our lives is the relationship that must be drawn and sustained if the church is to be perceived as more than simply another community service organization.[7]

As an older generation passes on its leadership of the church, these issues are crucial. At the present time, the financial support of the church is disproportionately carried by those who came of age in the 1940s and 1950s. If the church is to continue in any vital form, it must reach out to younger generations. This can happen only if the church is credible as a community of faith—if it offers something different from the standard clichés and moralisms of the dominant culture.[8] In this context, the "program" of the church emerges from Jesus' message of forgiveness and reconciliation. In the depths of this call to salvation lies the recognition that there is no personal conversion without discipleship. Conversely, the only authentic form of social ministry emerges from the recognition that what we "do unto others" is essentially what we need done for ourselves. The poor are not the objects of our charity, but partners in crafting a new humanity, a new vision of heaven and earth. These issues are central to our credibility "as servants of Christ and stewards of God's mysteries" (1 Cor. 4:1).

For Christians, the world is the place in which, and the place over against which, God calls each of us to responsibility. The human spirit is illuminated, freed, and empowered by the Holy Spirit—God—known in the world as hope, energy, imagination, and love. As Christians, we are called out of the Christian community for service in the larger society. The ministry of the laity (laos), in this sense, is the only real ministry of the church, for such are the people of God.

When Jesus said, "Come, and follow me," he did not lead his disciples into a church; he led them into the world. Or more to the point, the friends of Jesus became a church, a community of faith, called to serve and to lead in ministry to the world. Vocation, as Dietrich Bonhoeffer reminded us, is responsibility, and this is a call to men and women to "the whole of reality."[9] We live in a world of concrete situations where the affairs of states, the economics of the market, and the lives of individuals and families are mixed and tied together in a pluralistic society. If God is the God of the living and not the dead, then the world with all its counterpoints and cross-ings calls us to responsibility, to wonder, and to praise. The church should exist as a community of faith in behalf of this world; it is a sign and symbol of God's love for humanity. It is a place where our vocation as human beings is represented and interpreted. In the church we need to reclaim ministry for all Christians. The reduction of Christian vocation to the "full-time Christian service" of a few paid professional clergy makes faith a disembodied com-mitment that centers in feeling religious, but has little to do with thought and practice in everyday life. This is essentially the critique that Wendell Berry makes of churches that have given up the possi-bility of the diverse callings of all Christians. "The churches in this way," he writes, "excerpt sanctity from the human economy and its work just as Cartesian science has excerpted it from the material creation."[10] As he goes on to point out, the desecration of work is fundamentally tied to the desecration of nature. If there is nothing holy—no intrinsic purpose or service—embodied in the work we do, then it is easy to see that nature has no value either as God's handiwork. The severing of the tie between our work and our call-ing leads directly to the destruction of the land, sea, and air because they are there only to be used, not valued for their own sake. The natural world, therefore, has no worth apart from its economic worth, just as human beings are increasingly reduced in their sig-nificance to being "human resources."[11]

If there is any sense of calling left in many congregations, it is expressed in getting people involved in the programs of the church or in sending others to seminary to become clergy. We have turned things upside down. Clergy tend to focus almost solely on minister-ing to the needs of the congregation rather than equipping the con-gregation for ministry. The church then feeds on itself rather than being the bread of the world. In this context, vocation has no mean-ing except as service in behalf of the religious institution that, in effect, indicates we have rejected the Reformation of the sixteenth century and returned to the kind of medieval clericalism against which Luther mounted his protest. Ironically, in this attempt to "meet needs" what is missing is the central need of persons to find some way to balance work, personal life, and the larger world. We tend to think that we meet needs by drawing men and women into church programs that are almost entirely centered on the church's interests rather than seeing the church as the place in which the various strands of our lives may be perceived within some larger whole, giving a sense of purpose that helps us interpret and give priority to the various demands on our lives. Few people see their work as directly related to their Christian faith, yet the gospel affirms that in such public expressions of our lives we take up the particularities of our own calling—the ways in which our gifts, wounds, and circumstances are transformed by the purposes of God. This is the deepest need we can meet within the church.

The Protestant reformers knew that the priesthood of all believers is the radical edge of the gospel. The farther away we are from our calling in daily life and work, the more distant we are from knowing the power of God to transform human life. Vocation is the issue of how God shapes life and work into ways of thinking, acting, and willing in the name of Christ. It is the question of what difference it makes to believe at all.

In this context, a prayer of strength and beauty in *The Book of Common Prayer* of 1928 is a prayer about work and calling. The heart of the prayer reads: "Deliver us, we beseech thee, in our several callings, from the service of mammon, that we may do the work which thou givest us to do, in truth, in beauty, and in righteousness, with singleness of heart as thy servants, and to the benefit of our fellow men."[12] In the revision of the Prayer Book in 1977, this prayer for "our several callings" was changed to read: "Deliver us, we beseech thee, in our several occupations from the service of self alone, that we may do the work which thou givest us to do, in truth and beauty and for the common good."[13]

The shift from "our several callings" to "our several occupations" is a critical change. The idea of callings is reduced to the level of occupations without any apparent regard for the way callings involve far more than jobs. Wendell Berry wonders whether this prayer can be prayed at all in a society that recognizes little claim of truth, beauty, or goodness on the economic order. The distancing of persons from claims that have any transcendent reference establishes a situation in which only immediate, utilitarian, self-serving values have the power to persuade.[14]

Furthermore, the use of occupation in the prayer tends to isolate a sense of calling to church responsibilities; it makes ministry a separated, sacralized form of work; and it implies that only in specifically designated church work is there any room for work as a divine calling. In contrast with this reductionistic definition, Hans-Ruedi Weber asserts: "Christian work is mostly not something done in addition to our ordinary work, but it is ordinary work done with grace."[15]

In this sense, the congregation is called to be a place where we call one another to responsibility in our ordinary work. The shared life of prayer and thanksgiving, which is the center of church life, establishes the settings in which we do the work of discernment, where we are equipped to rethink the nature of all service in the world, the work we do, and the commitments we make with our time, gifts, and resources.

We cannot live only for this present time. God calls us to live not just for ourselves or the current generation, but in behalf of those who will follow us. This is the point of a story told by Gregory Bateson. A number of years ago, the oak beams in the dining hall of New College, Oxford, became infested with beetles and were deteriorating. The college head searched for suitable replacements for the beams, but none were to be found. Then a call was placed to the university forester to inquire if there were any oak trees that might be made into beams. In response, the forester explained that when New College was founded in 1379, a grove of oak trees had been planted to provide replacements for the beams when they eventually became infested with death watch beetles. The founders of the college knew that oak beams always need to be replaced because they had seen such beams infested with beetles. Their legacy had been handed down from generation to generation.[16]

Once while visiting Oxford, I stopped by the dining hall at New College. It was lunch time. The students were eating beneath the oak beams that spanned the ceiling. Not one of them was saying thanks in an obvious way, but in my mind's eye I could see the arms of those early founders stretched out over time into that space caring for a generation whose names and faces they could not know, but whose lives they continued to sustain. In similar ways, congregations need to see themselves extended in time and space—toward eternity.

TWELVE

~

Generosity of Spirit

Now faith is the assurance of things hoped for, the conviction of
things not seen.

—Hebrews 11:1

The demands of faith are absolute: we must put all our eggs in one
basket; we must burn our bridges.

—Wendell Berry, *Recollected Essays*[1]

FUNDAMENTAL CHANGE IN CONGREGATIONS, the movement toward renewal and reform, comes about through the conviction
of faithful people touched by the leading of God. It depends most
of all on individuals reconsidering expectations in light of what they
discern God might be calling them to be and do. I saw this firsthand
in my early years of pastoral ministry in Vermont.

On the village common in Strafford, Vermont, there is a classic
meeting house constructed in the late eighteenth century for worship and town gatherings. The building was used only for a few years
as a place of worship since the villagers soon divided into various
denominations that built their own churches around the edges of
the common or on down the road. When I first served the United
Church of Strafford in 1966, the Congregational and Baptist
Churches, which made up the United Church, had been together
for a number of years. The congregation was actually composed of
Congregationalists, a few Baptists, a number of Episcopalians, and
a faithful corps of Quakers. We worshiped for six months in one
church and then loaded candlesticks, cross, and hymnals in a pickup
truck and moved to the other for the next six. The pastoral role was
essentially that of minister to the whole community. Over the years,

the villages of Strafford and South Strafford had seen the rise and fall of population as the size of the town depended on the fortunes of the local copper mine. When the mine closed, many people left; those who remained made their living by farming and working in communities such as Hanover, New Hampshire, and White River Junction, Vermont. Over time new families moved to the village in order to begin another way of living from what they had experienced in more urban places. In late spring each year, church numbers doubled as "summer people" began returning to this place where they felt most of all at home.

Sometimes there are seasons of institutional life when things become possible that otherwise would lie dormant. What comes as possibility does not remain for long, and so it is important to discern the calling of the moment. In Strafford, I was privileged to see such a time of renewal in the life of the church. The two congregations that composed the United Church voted to form one ecumenical church related to the United Church of Christ and the American Baptists. The congregations essentially ended their separate identities in order to create a genuinely united church. What made this restructuring a moment of renewal, and not just an institutional rearrangement, was the decision of the deacons to require members to join the new church by reaffirming their faith and owning the church's covenant. There was no wholesale transfer of membership. This decision came out of long months of inquiry about the nature of the church, the meaning of ministry, and a sense of what God might be calling the church to become in this moment.

The foundation of this story of restructuring was a renewed commitment to the gospel and the search for ways of reconceiving the church's ministry as more than chaplaincy. The congregation saw its work as a work of faith in behalf of people in the community as well as in the larger world. In effect, the church sought to move to the crossroads of public life without any presumption of trying to reoccupy the center. The congregation engaged with issues surrounding the civil rights movement and began to look at the emerging questions of the Vietnam War. Members of the congregation opened their homes in the summer to children from the city, raised money to support the civil rights struggle, and became acquainted with members of the hippie commune on the edge of town who had been seen as a threat by some villagers. After a while, the new congregation decided that it would worship in the Congregational church and use the Baptist church building for education and community work. The congregation determined that its buildings were not museums for the display of memorabilia, but gathering places for a lively community of faith. Eventually, the church voted to give the Baptist building to the village for use as a gym.

One morning while the church was moving toward voting on the proposed change, I got a telephone call from the leader of the Congregational church's Ladies Benevolent Circle. She indicated that the group had met and wanted to speak with me right away. While I was curious about what they might want to talk about, I was somewhat unnerved about their imminent arrival on the porch of the parsonage. It was a processional of no small significance. Actually, there were two women's groups, one in the Baptist church and one in the Congregational, and they were centers of opinion and power in the community. My first guess was that the phone call meant that, one way or the other, a line was being drawn regarding the impending church vote.

When the group arrived, what they had to say was that they had talked about the plans for the new church, and the more they talked, the more they felt that the women's groups needed to take the lead. They were proposing the formation of a unified women's group for the two communities to signal support for the new venture. It was the stuff of which revolutions are made and a gift no long-range planning committee could ever have concocted. Theirs was a proposal too unpredictable for rational explanation. Generations of denominational rivalry, subtle class conflict, and family disputes were overwhelmed in this moment by a generosity of spirit that can be explained only by the grace of God. Too often we think of restructuring as a logical and objective process. My experience is that for change to occur in anything that matters, it has to be built on faith expressed in such acts of generosity.

THIRTEEN

~

Large Things in a Small Parish

But we have this treasure in clay jars, so that it may be made clear
that this extraordinary power belongs to God and does not come
from us.

—2 Corinthians 4:7

You are messengers of God's truth clothed in the beauty of God.
Take hope ... and hold up the glory of the heavenly city.

—Paul Moore, *Presences*[1]

PROTESTANT CHURCHES ARE FOUNDED on the assumption that
the church is always reforming. There is no sanctified place, no
safe spot where we can settle down and build our own version of
the realm of God. Instead, we affirm that faith is a journey—a pilgrimage. This is the predominant image of the faithful life. It means
we travel light and know that God calls us to respond rather than
rationalize and defend. In this regard, one of the most difficult issues facing some congregations is how to find different models of
leadership when the professional model of full-time, ordained clergy
is neither possible nor even necessarily faithful. Consider the story
of St. Stephen and the Incarnation, an Episcopal parish in Washington, D.C., which is sometimes known as St. Stephen and the In-
surrection because of its reputation as a prophetic congregation.
For many years, the church was led by the Rev. William Wendt, who
was a well-known leader in the civil rights struggle, the protest
against the war in Vietnam, and other social causes. The church has
carved out a distinctive niche in the ecclesiastical world of Washington, and it has attracted as well as lost members because of this
identity.

In the 1960s, St. Stephen's had a membership of nearly a thousand; now it is a congregation of 100 to 125 persons. What strikes a visitor is the diversity of the worshiping community. It is one of the few genuinely multicultural congregations in the United States. The worship tends toward high church Anglicanism, but paradoxically, the style is informal and inclusive. The church building looks somewhat like a National Guard armory on the outside, but within, the church is a place of striking, almost offbeat, beauty. Many of the fixed pews have been removed and the space designed in a way more akin to a cathedral than a local church. The congregation is fully involved in the liturgy, and there is an ease with the movement of worship that only a few congregations achieve. During the prayers of the people, the joys and concerns of the congregation extend for a lengthy time as lives are shared and attention focused beyond the confines of the church's internal preoccupations.

At present, there is no full-time rector or pastor. The church is led by elected lay leaders, who have been authorized by the bishop to oversee the life of the parish. The congregation calls on the volunteer services of several ordained clergy, who have some association with the parish. These clergy alternate in preaching, providing pastoral care, and celebrating the eucharist on Sunday. The designation of worship leader for the Sunday service, however, is assigned to one of the members of the church, and the liturgy itself reflects this sense of leadership and participation. The parish is not quite sure what it wants regarding professional leadership. Some members think it is time to call a full-time pastor. Others feel the church should continue without such a full-time professional. In the meantime, the parish has put on hold some of the pressing issues of restructuring and maintenance, which cannot be held off indefinitely.

The issues facing St. Stephen's are familiar ones in many congregations. The parish may have a higher public profile than most, and it does have a number of theologically educated leaders, but fundamentally, the issues it faces are common issues in any small church. Most obvious of these issues is the question of whether the parish can afford a full-time professional minister. Hiring one would mean cutting back on other commitments, and in the perspective of many congregants, it would also undercut the leadership of the congregation itself. Ideally, the role of the pastor is to equip the ministry of the congregation, but in practice, some members of St. Stephen's feel that this often means the focus is on the pastor's ministry rather than the people's.

The church is able to get by financially with individual contributions and income from renting space to various community service organizations. Adding a clerical salary would constitute a budget imbalance. It is generally recognized, though, that even if the congregation does not call a full-time pastor, the church needs some kind of permanent staff. On a surface level, this indicates a business manager, but on a more imaginative level, it suggests something more than this. The church, in the opinion of many, needs someone who is able to sustain initiatives and organize the work of the parish. This is new work because the choices usually faced by small churches are to get bigger, to close down, or to get by with part-time assistance. What St. Stephen's struggles to envision is a new model that calls out the leadership of the congregation, yet takes seriously the hard and sustained work needed "to equip the saints for the work of ministry, for building up the body of Christ" (Eph. 4:12).

Part of the difficulty of St. Stephen's is the absence of working models of congregational leadership other than the full-time clerical one. Having grown accustomed to Christendom, we inherit an ecclesiastical model that tends to make clergy the essential definition of the church. Sometimes we act as if the congregation's sole vocation is to support a full-time pastor. This assumes, of course, that the primary purpose of clergy is to meet the individual needs of the congregation as a permanent and resident chaplain. However, when a congregation claims its vocation in ministry, it is called as well to envision the kinds of authorized ministries and leaders it needs to discern and embody this vocation. In the future, we must design diverse models of leadership, which will include ordained ministers of Word and sacrament; but the models will also include men and women authorized in ministry as directors of parish life, missioners, stewardship officers, and teachers.

I have in mind a reorientation of leadership in smaller congregations, to be provided by men and women who have been called to pastoral ministry and who have completed theological studies, but who are not dependent on the church for their livelihood. This approach to leadership permits the congregation to see the budget as an expression of mission rather than as the fiscal support of one ministry, namely, pastoral ministry to themselves. I think there are faithful and gifted persons for whom this kind of ministry is a significant calling and not a reduced understanding of pastoral leadership, as is now the case. At the same time, we need to consider the possibility of other models that focus on indigenous leadership within congregations that are not based on a clerical model. Congregations composed of twenty or thirty members can be energetic communities of faith with leadership that understands the vitality of such base communities. Leaders raised up from within the congregation can be equipped for ministry by cooperative educational ventures of denominations and theological schools.

All of the questions facing St. Stephen's are pursued within the fundamental assumption that the congregation is most of all defined by its location in Columbia Heights, an urban neighborhood often overlooked and forgotten. The church building itself, for which there is great affection, calls a congregation to worship that is deeply connected to its mission in the community. The location of St. Stephen's, in this sense, is the major clue to its vocation. This is made clear in a brief history of the parish that ends with the fundamental question, "How is St. Stephen's the church in this neighborhood? It is already one of the best community centers in town, but how is it the church?"[2]

The simplest solution for St. Stephen's is not to make any clear decisions at all. Unfortunately, this approach is often taken by small congregations that are proud of getting by and muddling through. In effect, the decision not to decide defines the small congregation as a failed large church. The future for such a church is usually a slow decline as membership dwindles, resources erode, and costs finally become too prohibitive to continue.

St. Stephen's wants to chart a different course, and it wrestles now with imagining a congregational model that sustains the gifts and values of being relatively small, yet does not shrink from its larger calling. It is the vocation that the poet and priest R. S. Thomas once affirmed when he said, "I was vicar of large things / in a small parish."[3] In this regard, St. Stephen's faces important questions that many congregations share:

- How can a small congregation find a distinctive way of being a church that is not simply a pale imitation of a larger church?

- How does such a congregation take seriously the need for pastoral care and theological formation without necessarily adopting a full-time clerical model?

- How does a small church determine the kind of permanent, sustained leadership that is needed to care for and build up the church's institutional responsibilities? What are the organizational structures required for this kind of leadership?

- How does a congregation initiate a process of discernment that allows it to hear God's calling in this present and future moment? How is this process open to new ideas that challenge the church to rethink its expectations and to hear a calling that might be surprising and unexpected?

- What is required for the church to see itself as fellowship (*koinonia*) and as institution (*ekklesia*) and to deal with the kind of conflict that emerges in the midst of making fundamental decisions about these forms of church life?[4]

There are no easy answers to these questions, but a congregation that has the courage and fidelity to live within such questions is a congregation that will be claimed by answers it may now dimly perceive. Moreover, the answers found by one church will not necessarily be solutions that are applicable to another. In this regard, we are often bound by images of nailed down church structures that do not convey the movable and changing models that have been part of our history.

In one sense, the story of the early Christian movement is a search for structures of organization and leadership that expressed the Spirit's presence in the midst of diverse and often cantankerous congregations. We tend to look back at such congregations as Corinth, Philippi, and Rome with a fixed gaze that misses the extent to which those communities of faith were constantly dealing with pressing issues of form and mission. It is hard work, but it is the crucial work of the church, understanding that "we have this treasure in clay jars." Everything except the gospel is provisional, for the power of the gospel belongs to God and not to us.

FOURTEEN

~

Communion

Now you are the body of Christ and individually members of it.

—1 Corinthians 12:27

[Our participation in church] . . . began from a social feeling, but moved on—from community to communion.

—Donald Hall, *Paris Review*[1]

ALTHOUGH THE CHURCH is a broken and hesitant witness to the gospel, it has been called to proclaim what it cannot always embody. In the midst of this community made up of all the promises and pitfalls of being human, there is from time to time a sense of communion that comes by God's grace. In 1990, I was reading the poet Donald Hall's *Here at Eagle Pond* and found that he and his wife, poet Jane Kenyon, were leaders in the South Danbury Christian Church in New Hampshire. He spoke of how they had first gone to the small country church that had been part of the traditions of his family for many generations because "*they*—probably the dead— would expect us to go to church. . . . Wearily we dragged ourselves there the first Sunday; the second Sunday we went less wearily; within a few weeks we got there early."[2] They were surprised and pleased that on that first day in church, the minister referred to Rainer Maria Rilke, but the quote from the German poet was not the crucial point of "turning them into deacons." They were moved to a deeper level of commitment when what "started with community . . . extended itself to communion."[3]

For some time I thought about what I had read, and I was interested in learning more about the poets' experience in church. Partly out of shyness, but mostly out of a sense that poets and monks deserve their privacy, I did not follow up on my curiosity, but let it lie in the back of my mind. Since South Danbury is not far from Hanover, New Hampshire, where Bangor Seminary had begun some programs in theological education, I was in the area on a regular basis. When I was in the community, I often thought of Donald Hall, Jane Kenyon, and the South Danbury Church. One day, Alice Ling, who was directing a project in congregational leadership for the seminary, gave me a letter she had just received from Donald Hall. She had recently preached in the South Danbury Church to help out while the congregation was searching for a minister, and he was writing to ask if she would consider becoming their pastor. Whether it was coincidence, providence, or whatever, I took it as a gift and worked with Alice Ling to create a way that we could covenant with the congregation so that she served the South Danbury Church as part of her responsibilities as a member of the faculty and staff of the seminary.

A few years later, during an evening at the Church of Christ at Dartmouth College, also in Hanover, Jane Kenyon and Donald Hall read poems that had emerged from their lives in the South Danbury congregation. It was an evening of extraordinary grace, a testimony to faith, and an appreciation of the ministries of Jack Jensen, who had served the church for many years before his death, and of Alice Ling, who was now their pastor.

Speaking more directly about their relationship with the church, Donald Hall affirmed: "It is true community came before communion did, but the community was Christian and it led toward communion with the help of our then-minister [Jack Jensen]."[4] In particular, Jack Jensen helped them think about Scripture and the writings of mystics and theologians—"adding thought to feeling."[5] In this same vein, Jane Kenyon spoke:

> Well, Don and I really began going to this little church as a sort of cultural exercise. It was part of community life there. I certainly never thought that I wanted or needed to be "ministered unto." It never would have occurred to me that I needed these things. But in hearing Jack's sermons week after week, I found he was learned. I respected his mind. I respected his intelligence and I really began to

listen, and in his sermons I heard about a God who was very different from the one I had learned about from my grandmother. . . . I was surprised by a belief in my early thirties. I was utterly astonished.[6]

In reflecting on his journey in faith, Donald Hall remembers that at the age of twelve he had what he terms "the atheist conversion."[7] He realized that Lot's wife probably did not turn into a pillar of salt, and that recognition pulled him away from the church and any religious commitment. Over the years he sometimes went to church, but he attended for aesthetic reasons—for the music and architecture. "It took me a long time to figure out," he writes, "that there were other things that I was after and it took me, in fact, coming back to New Hampshire, the place where we live, to find out."[8] The church in which his own faith was reawakened was not significant architecturally, and the music hardly up to the standards of cathedral choristers; but in that small rural church in South Danbury, Donald Hall rediscovered the traditions of faith, or more particularly, he was reclaimed by the gospel.

His learning in the gospel began with a new belonging to a distinctive community that kept alive the story of Jesus. The small New Hampshire congregation was a place of learning because, in that community, there was a center of belief that was evident in the life of the church. This is important for us to remember. What attracts, converts, and compels people to stay in a congregation is the congregation's witness as the body of Christ. The church is not a community without definition; it is Christ's body, and this is what Donald Hall and Jane Kenyon came to recognize in their belonging to that gathering of believers.

In the movement from belonging to believing, a sense of community came first, then communion. The relationship was shaped by the common tie with the figure of Jesus, who was in the midst of that congregation's common life—the stuff of church fairs, potluck suppers, Sunday school pageants, shared suffering, and deep joy. What deepened the initial feelings of community and transposed them to another level of understanding and commitment was the way in which Jack Jensen shared the traditions of faith and helped the congregation think about their lives in light of the gospel's peculiar angle of seeing the world. He taught what he knew of the biblical narratives and shared the ups and downs of his life in faith. But in the discipline of his calling, he got out of the way and became a means of bringing into view the presence of Jesus, who was the essential teacher. The members of the South Danbury congregation prayed together, cared for one another, and paid attention to the call of the larger world. As teacher, Jack Jensen helped the community of faith draw upon the traditions that had formed it and continued to renew its life. As Donald Hall and Jane Kenyon observed, he "added his learning to a sense of community that was already there."[9]

In looking at Jane Kenyon's poetry, in particular, we can see this continuing struggle with faith and experience. Her poetry looks without blinking at the hard as well as the graceful realities of our lives. All of her life, Jane Kenyon faced severe depression, the "Unholy ghost" that returned again and again:

> Pharmaceutical wonders are at work
> but I believe only in this moment
> of well-being. Unholy ghost,
> you are certain to come again.[10]

She moved through depression with the help of loved ones, antidepressants, and the grace of ordinary things that bring hope:

> White peonies blooming along the porch
> send out light
> while the rest of the yard grows dim.[11]

In Jesus' life, Jane Kenyon found One who understood the depths of suffering and the nature of grace, an earthy figure who was no figment of imagination or disembodied spirit. This is the focus of "Looking at Stars":

> The God of curved space, the dry
> God, is not going to help us, but the son
> whose blood spattered
> the hem of his mother's robe.[12]

Perhaps the deepest statement of faith is the poem "Let Evening Come," which was written shortly after a Maundy Thursday communion service. The story of Jesus' last supper with his disciples, his betrayal by one of them, and the suffering toward which he turned his face is the background of the poem. Unlike writers of typical religious poetry that makes the point so obvious as to trivialize the subject, Jane Kenyon does the hard work of transposition. The poem signals that we live in a world of fragile commitments, a world of uncertainty, but we live also with the promise of what lies ahead. In the grace of ordinary things, we see redemption. We see the "light of late afternoon," "the cricket take up chafing," "dew collect on the hoe abandoned in long grass," "the bottle in the ditch," and "air in the lung." Most of all, in this seeing, we can finally say:

> Let it come, as it will, and don't
> be afraid. God does not leave us
> comfortless, so let evening come.[13]

Jane Kenyon died in April 1995, at home on Eagle Pond. She had gone to a hospital in Seattle, Washington, in a final effort to halt the leukemia that had wracked her body for months. Nothing worked, and finally, she threw away all the medications and faced the end of the struggle with family and friends who were her companions in those final days. She completed the collection of her poems later published as *Otherwise*, and she worked on a poem, "The Sick Wife." Her funeral was in the South Danbury Church, where she had been astonished to find faith.

Donald Hall endured the deep grief of Jane's death. He wrote letters to her, visited her grave, spoke with her about the weather, and passed on news of friends and family. He noticed her peonies, the same ones she had written about:

> Your peonies burst out, white as snow squalls,
> with red flecks at their shaggy centers
> in your border of prodigies by the porch.
> I carry one magnanimous blossom indoors
> and float it in a glass bowl, as you used to do.[14]

Mostly, however, days were lived without the hopeful presence of peonies:

> In hell. Every day
> I play in repertory the same
> script without you, without love,
> without audience except for Gus,
> who waits attentive
> for cues: a walk, a biscuit,
> bedtime. The year of days
> without you and your body swept by
> as quick as an afternoon;
> but each afternoon took a year.[15]

Church was not a place of habitation during those months and days. The sojourn in flatness and pain continued, but another Easter did come and a return to the community gathered in the South Danbury Church. Perhaps Jane Kenyon had anticipated all of this in her own thought about promise and hope, beyond suffering and despair, in "Notes from the Other Side":

> I divested myself of despair
> and fear when I came here ...
> and God, as promised, proves
> to be mercy clothed in light.[16]

The story of Donald Hall and Jane Kenyon and their life as poets in the church is an expression of the kind of shift that has to occur if the gospel is to make any difference in our lives. Thus our attempt to reclaim the Christian faith in the midst of the skepticism of liberal Protestant churches depends largely on how we address the matter of biblical interpretation. The fundamentalist-modernist controversies of the early twentieth century left many Protestants with the suspicion that faith was not seemly. In a manner almost as literal as that of the fundamentalists, many liberal Protestants saw the critique of scriptural inerrancy as proof that the whole religious tradition was bogus. The only things left for them were a set of ideals, clues for the good life, and perhaps some stories for children. The next steps in interpretation never got made: exploring the nature of faith, recognizing who it is that claims our lives, and how the stories of the gospel have authority for us.

Donald Hall's turn away from faith, when he decided that Lot's wife may not have ended up a pillar of salt, is a moment replicated in many different ways as young people, in particular, begin to raise questions about the language of faith. In a similar way, Jane Kenyon's dismissal of the God described by her grandmother left her with a residue of resentment and pain that made faith a distant and questionable reality. Jack Jensen made the traditions of the Christian faith available to them once again and encouraged their basic learning of the gospel. It was not a matter of translating the gospel so that it fit acceptable categories of thinking; rather, it was offering the gospel as another way of seeing the world and allowing this new sight to make a difference in their lives.

Jack Jensen's work was not to try to create an experience of God, which is too often the task for which clergy see themselves responsible. Instead, he affirmed what difference Christian belief makes in our lives, the nature of Christ's presence in the world, and the diverse ways in which Christians have understood the gospel over the centuries. Obviously, poets such as Donald Hall and Jane Kenyon already know about the nature of metaphor and the connecting of thought with feeling, but their experience is fundamentally similar to ours. All who say yes to Christ engage in the continuing task of interpreting and reinterpreting experience in light of the gospel. Teaching is, therefore, an essential practice of pastoral ministry so that the stories of God may be told and the congregation engaged in the common learning that lies at the heart of the church—the journey from community to communion.

PART FOUR

Serving and Leading

~

You don't always get exactly where you meant to go. It is a question of balancing forces that are constantly changing, possibilities that continually transmute. Still there is that moment always hoped for, when everything conjoins and the boat leaps forward, creating its own wind, apparent wind exceeding true wind, drawing the boat onward.

—Susan Kenney, *Sailing*[1]

FIFTEEN

~

Leaders Deep Down Inside

I am among you as one who serves.

—Luke 22:27

To lead is to go out ahead and show the way when the way may be unclear, difficult, or dangerous—it is not just walking at the head of the parade.

—Robert K. Greenleaf, *The Servant as Religious Leader*[1]

IF CONGREGATIONS ARE TO FIND new life, leadership is crucial; but what is leadership, and how is it practiced? These are questions I connect most of all with Robert K. Greenleaf, whom I first met through his book *Servant Leadership: A Journey into the Nature of Legitimate Power and Greatness*.[2] For many years, Bob Greenleaf was an in-house consultant for AT&T serving in different roles as teacher, advisor, and occasional speech writer. Most of all, he was concerned with how AT&T and other organizations actually worked. At the same time, he read widely and leaned toward the Quaker faith and practice. Early in his career Bob decided that when he became sixty, he would retire from corporate life in order to work as a consultant to nonprofit institutions, colleges, and universities. In his later years he worked increasingly with churches and theological seminaries.

Over the years, I met with him for what became a continuing seminar on leadership and the nature of institutions. He was a teacher and a tough mentor in his own soft-spoken way. There was plenty of idealism in Bob Greenleaf, but little sentimentality. He was encouraging, yet unrelenting in not allowing any retreat from reality. In particular, he helped me see that regardless of how much we might want to define leadership on our own terms, the fact is that the distinctive needs of a school, church, or any other organization create the setting in which the actual form of leadership is shaped. What we might like to do could be interesting and important, but it could also be very much beside the point of the leadership that is called for in a particular moment of institutional life. The hard edge of leadership is recognizing and accepting the cost of the work you may be called to do. This takes insight, no little courage and, most of all, faith.

Leadership centers in the care of the people who make up an organization and the mission of the organization itself. It focuses on the development of a shared vision through the continuing analysis and interpretation of the assumptions on which an organization bases its work. It pays attention to the systems and connections that comprise the culture of the institution. Obviously, the kind of leadership that Robert Greenleaf calls us to consider is transformative. This work of leadership is to help the people of an institution discern their calling and envision what it means for organizational life. Bob used the word "lead" in the sense of going "out ahead to show the way" rather than in the more typical focus on administration and management. Neither maintenance of the status quo nor coercive or manipulative tactics to achieve goals had anything to do with what he perceived as leadership.[3] Leading, in his view, has to do with courage and risk. It requires the willingness to live within the vision of a new possibility, but it insists on the patience to let that vision unfold and by its own power persuade others to follow in that direction. In this regard, leadership at the deepest levels is a matter of Spirit.[4]

One of the most common stereotypes of leadership is the image of the enthusiastic troop leader—a kind of corporate cheerleader conducting group building exercises before the doors open at Wal-Mart. On a more sophisticated level, the image is that of the motivational seminar for executives, which is characterized by leadership posed with unrelenting good humor and positive appeal. There is nothing wrong with good humor or positive appeal, but neither necessarily has much to do with leadership rooted in spirituality.

Instead of enthusiasm, Robert Greenleaf suggests that we should bring back into usage the word *entheos*, which means "possessed of the spirit." We more commonly employ "enthusiasm," which originally had the connotation of being a more superficial form of *entheos*. *Entheos* refers to the fundamental spirit that informs our sense of self, provides energy, permits us to go beyond our own self-imposed boundaries, and helps us connect our individual concerns with public issues. In a theological perspective, *entheos* is a gift of the Holy Spirit, which gives us life; it is the energy and imagination of God that can redeem our outworn images and tepid commitments.[5]

The primary level of leadership is at the level of vocation: the basic calling of the institution. For religious institutions, this sometimes suggests a form of long-range planning that has little to do with the life of the organization itself. We dream of what we would like to be and create a long list of goals that are far removed from the reality of the institution we serve. To consider vocation, however, is to deal with the actual context and to trust that, within this setting, God calls us to discern the vision and the mission out of which we will shape the work of the institution. This means struggling with the reality of the institution, looking at its data, testing the quality of its service, and reading all this information as a clue to what God might be saying, even if the message is one we do not want to hear.[6]

The work of leadership is a matter of living within questions that raise the issue of vocation. There are essentially four persisting questions:

1. Who are we and where did we come from?
2. Where are we going?
3. What will it take to get us there?
4. How will we know how we are doing?

These are basic, strategic questions. Given the unpredictable economic and social climate in which organizations now have to function, these questions help an institution pay attention to its context and constituency. A fifth question that might be added to the basic four is one that Robert Greenleaf often asked of organizations, "Who would miss you if you no longer existed?"

The constant temptation of all institutions, especially religious ones, is the desire to be something other than what they are called to become. Instead of looking at the uniqueness of the mission that is ours, we tend to imitate existing models and try to transplant those ideal models to our own organizations. More and more we try to do all sorts of things that we have seen other institutions do successfully, only to find that we do not do them very well at all. In the effort to imitate, we lose sight of the distinctive vocation given to us by God.

A primary responsibility of leadership, then, is to see that the continuing inquiry into the nature and purpose of the institution is sustained and supported. It is not the leader's responsibility to answer all the questions, but it is the leader's task to maintain the institution's ongoing conversation about things that matter—its fidelity to the vision and the people it serves. Most important, this level of leadership is expressed in telling the story of the institution, interpreting its history, and searching for the metaphors and symbols that embody its vision and mission.[7] The best theologies and theories of leadership have always known that organizations are communities of learning and that teaching is the central role of leadership. Reflecting this wisdom, Wendell Berry writes, "Like a good farmer, a good teacher is the trustee of a vital and delicate organism: the life of the mind in his community. The ultimate and defining standard of his discipline is his community's health and intelligence and coherence and endurance. This is a high calling, deserving of a life's work."[8]

In this regard, Robert Greenleaf saw that the leader's work is essentially that of equipping the members of an organization for the work of discerning the vision that calls it to life. It is the effort to help an organization recognize the reality in which it lives and the ways in which that reality calls the institution to rethink its purpose and reexamine its practices. This is shared work that requires a sense of collaboration and mutuality.[9] In the center of this work is the effort to understand the nature of an organization's culture—its ways of sustaining what it values, the forms through which it expresses these values, and the networks of relationship that give life and expression to its purpose. Most of all, it has to do with the ethos and the ethics of the institution—its fidelity to the people and the purposes it serves.

A few years ago, I was on retreat at the Abbey of Gethsemani, the Trappist monastery near Bardstown, Kentucky. At an early morning service, I heard one of the monks begin a homily with the words: "If you take your life seriously, it has style." The kind of style that the Trappist monk was referring to has nothing to do with fads or fashion; rather, it refers to the cultivation of an ordered life that comes from faithfulness to purposes that shape our commitments and form our practices of work and relationship. Style, in an institutional sense, refers to cultivating a distinctive way of being that clearly expresses the purposes of the organization.

It is difficult to think of this sense of style in regard to institutions. We know that institutions have a character and a culture, but mostly, we see these elements as something given and inherited. Seldom do we consider that we need to cultivate and nurture the style of the institution. The fact is that without an intentional sense of attention to the forms and symbols of institutional life, the culture of a congregation will change in often unintended ways over time. The nature of policies, governing ideas, symbols, and vision are central to the institution's style of life. The inquiry into this foundational level of institutional life is the responsibility of the whole institution, but especially it is the teaching office of the leader.

Anyone who has experienced this kind of leadership knows that it is a complex affair. It is one thing to crunch numbers, pass resolutions telling others what to do, or make sure the institution is running smoothly. It is quite another to raise questions about the relationship between the institution's purposes and its practices. It is one thing to respond to the pressure of an interest group; it is something else to keep diverse voices at the same table. The question finally comes down to what defines that sense of the whole and how the institution is formed by the whole rather than the sum total of its parts. Leadership that initiates and sustains this kind of inquiry is best characterized as prophetic. It is not a matter of predicting what lies ahead; rather, it is the question of where we are going if we continue in the direction we are currently moving. What are the values and commitments that shape our use of resources as well as all the decisions we make along the way? Ultimately, this kind of questioning examines the vision out of which these questions are raised and the practices that express the purposes of the institution.

Much of the time this kind of leadership is hard, quiet, and relatively anonymous work. It is the preparatory work of attending to the needs of the institution; it is the work of equipping committees to look at the policies for which they are responsible; and it is the task of gathering the data that can be transposed into usable information. Most of all, it is the unrelenting search for ways to raise in one way or another the most important question of all: How closely in our practices do we approximate the purposes for which we say we exist?

Often the experience of leadership is lonely and isolated. The hope expressed by Bob Greenleaf is that leadership is shared. Our experience informs us that this is seldom the case. Much of the time, all of the time for some, leadership is a solo, not an ensemble, effort. Underlying this isolation is the basic mythology of leadership, which portrays the leader as a unique individual who is given authority by members of a group in exchange for being relieved of their problems. In the end, this mythology is played out by the group taking back its authority, changing leaders, and repeating the play endlessly.[10] The fact is that no one has all the answers to the questions that emerge in institutional life, so, by necessity, leadership is a mutual responsibility. Because we cannot wait until ideal solutions come into view, we are called in faith to respond to the issues that face us even though we can never know for sure how things will turn out. What sustains our energy and rekindles our imagination should be a sense of trust in the promise of God, who calls us to participate in the continuing creation of the world.

Leadership, then, in the community of Jesus Christ is the servant ministry of those called to live in the Spirit and in the forms of hope that bring new energy and imagination to the institutions, movements, and occasions in which we lead, serve, and follow. Bob Greenleaf rediscovered the power of this image of leadership through a story by Herman Hesse. In *The Journey to the East*, Hesse tells the story of Leo, a servant to a group of pilgrims who are trying to find their way to the center of a religious order. Leo looks after the needs of the group and enlivens them with his stories and songs. The journey continues on its way until Leo leaves the group. Then the pilgrims are thrown into confusion, and the journey ends, for they cannot continue without the servant, Leo. Years later, one of the group, who is also the teller of the story, is taken to the place where the pilgrims had been headed. Here at the center of the order he finds that Leo, the servant, turns out to be the leader of the order itself.

In reflecting on this story, Bob writes, "This story clearly says— *the great leader is seen as servant first*, and that simple fact is the key to his greatness. Leo was actually the leader all of the time, but he was servant first because that was what he was, *deep down inside.*"[11]

SIXTEEN

~

The Silence of Prayer and the Voice of Ministry

Therefore, since it is by God's mercy that we are engaged in this
ministry, we do not lose heart.

—2 Corinthians 4:1

What many preachers say about the Mystery of God is often
lifeless and therefore ineffectual. What they say comes only from
words jumbled up with many thousands of other words. It does
not come from silence.

—Max Picard, *The World of Silence*[1]

THROUGHOUT THESE REFLECTIONS, I have claimed that the ministry (the discipleship) of all the people of God is an essential
mark of the church. At the same time, it is important to think about
the nature of ordained ministry and to look at the particular ministry of pastors and teachers in the church who are authorized "to
equip the saints for the work of ministry, for building up the body
of Christ" (Eph. 4:12).

The church, has required throughout its history that candidates
for ministry should be persons of Christian commitment, express a
sense of being called by God, demonstrate the intellectual and personal gifts required for leadership in a given time and circumstance,
and be chosen to serve a congregation or institution of the church.
Traditionally, these criteria have been termed, respectively, the call
to discipleship, the secret call, the providential call, and the ecclesiastical call.[2]

While this description of call has usually been focused on the
ordained ministry of the pastor and teacher, it is possible to apply
these categories to a broader understanding of ministry. Only the

ecclesiastical call actually requires ordination as a prerequisite for service. The call to discipleship, the secret call, and the providential call describe as well the ministry of the whole people of God, the laity (*laos*). In expanding the categories beyond ordained ministers, we broaden their application to a renewed sense of ministry as the vocation of all Christians.

First of all, the call to ministry is basically the call to discipleship. It is a summoning by God to see where we live and work as a place of ministry; or as is sometimes the case, it is the leading of God to other places and means of service. In baptism we are given all the recognition we will ever need to minister in the world. By water and by word, we are called to live as people of hope amid struggles where the power of life contends with the powers of death and destruction. This is not something we are invited to do in our spare time; it is at the center of our lives.

If we hear the call of God, if we can understand that what we need is not always what we desire, then we are invited to share Christ's ministry. Several years ago, I was worshiping in the Jubilee Community of the Church of the Saviour in Washington, D.C., which was uniquely formed around the mission commitment of its members. The Jubilee Community gathered on Monday evenings in the Potter's House, a coffee house the community ran in a marginal area of the city. During the service, a woman asked the congregation to pray for her since she was returning to her home in Mississippi and to members of her family she had not seen in thirty-five years. Later, I found out that the woman, now a leader in that community, had previously been an alcoholic living on the street. One night she went into the Potter's House, and some members of the congregation welcomed her. From that time, her life was never the same, as she was called by name and summoned to service through that community of faith.

In addition to this basic call to discipleship, there is also a secret call, which is a compelling inner understanding that God calls us to a particular kind of ministry. We begin to see that the things we do have their deepest significance as they are given in service to others and to the needs of the world. If we pay attention to these clues, then we may discover calling at a deeper level.

A physician I once met considered becoming an ordained minister. As she dealt with this possibility, she felt called to look at the elements of her life in a new way. Instead of moving toward ordination, though, she moved toward an understanding of ministry as it was revealed in her life. She rediscovered her calling as a physician whose gifts were not merely for her own fulfillment, but should be directed to the needs of the world as well. In all probability, she would have made a fine pastor, but the fact is that she was called to be a gifted physician. As a result of this sense of call, she gave up a lucrative position in order to establish a research clinic for children in a poor and conflict-filled part of the world.

Along with the call to discipleship and the secret call, a calling is made possible by intellectual and personal gifts shaped by the historical moment and the intersection of self and society. The life of Martin Luther King Jr. reflects such a providential sense of call. After completing doctoral studies in theology at Boston University, Dr. King accepted the pastorate of Dexter Avenue Baptist Church in Montgomery, Alabama, on April 15, 1954. He had gone to the university with the hope that someday he would become a professor, but he knew that he needed to establish himself first as a pastor. On May 17 of that same year, the Supreme Court handed down its judgment on the *Brown* vs. *Board of Higher Education* case. The highest court in the United States unanimously declared school segregation unconstitutional. While the full impact of the court's decision was not immediately obvious to the new pastor, his call to ministry was fundamentally changed by this landmark legal development. As a result, the course of his life was radically redirected. The gifts that would have made him a pastor or theologian were transformed by his call to a prophetic role. The ruling on segregation set events in motion that swept him down a path he never could have invented; it called him to a prophetic task for which he would ultimately give his life.[3]

At the height of the Montgomery boycott, King was uncertain about his role and his calling. He was exhausted and afraid of the events around him. One night he prayed, "Oh Lord . . . I'm down here trying to do what is right. But, Lord I must confess that I'm weak now. I'm afraid. The people are looking to me for leadership, and if I stand before them without strength and courage, they too will falter. I am at the end of my power. I have nothing left. I can't face it alone." In the silence of that moment, King heard another voice speaking to him: "Martin Luther, stand up for righteousness. Stand up for justice. Stand up for truth. And, lo, I will be with you, even unto the end of the world." At that point he knew that Christ would not abandon him, and that his vocation as a leader was embodied in the struggle of his people for freedom.[4]

Finally, there is the ecclesiastical call. This is the easiest to determine: either you do or do not have a letter of call from a pastoral search committee or agency of the church. A call from one of the institutional forms of the church is an invitation to take up the work of ministry in a particular community of Jesus Christ. Ordination does not set us aside in a special category of being; it authorizes us for the specific task of equipping the church for ministry.[5] Men and women are called to be pastors, teachers, and leaders in order for the church to discern its vocation as the body of Christ. Ordained ministers need to be Christians who understand the power of God's presence, know the church's traditions of faith, and are able to share these traditions through faithful and imaginative teaching. At the heart of this teaching is the effort to perceive the contemporary relevance of our traditions as they engage the alienation and suffering of the world.

While most ordained persons serve as pastors and teachers of local congregations, men and women are also ordained for service in specialized ministries such as theological education, rural and urban mission, pastoral care, denominational leadership, and institutional chaplaincies. In addition, most denominations provide for some form of commissioning or licensing to particular forms of service that may be long-term or short-term, but do not require ordination. The pastoral office of the ordained minister is to equip men and women for ministry or, as the letter to the Ephesians says, "to equip the saints for the work of ministry, for building up the body of Christ" (4:12). To be a pastor and teacher of the church is to be a local theologian who helps a congregation interpret its calling and engage in its mission. As a leader, the ordained minister serves a congregation that should be a place of worship, a community of teaching, and a company of prophetic witnesses.

Since ministry is not a solitary vocation, the process of discerning our place in ministry is essential. The committees of the church that review candidates for ordination are the primary means through which this may occur. Part of what this process helps us understand is the way we are chosen and the ways we choose ministry. Our sense of being called grows as we recognize the various elements that have shaped our calling. In this regard, God does not work in private. The instrument of God's revelation is our humanity. We find it hard to believe that God could choose us because we know the limited nature of our lives. But this transformation of lives embodies God's amazing grace, and we need the help of other Christians in discerning the presence of God in our lives as we interpret our sense of calling to ordained ministry.[6]

The hardest aspect of calling is being able to hear a "no" as well as a "yes" to our judgments about where we are called in ministry. Therefore, we should not try to interpret our calling by ourselves. We need help in clarifying and understanding the ways in which we are shaped by the purposes of God. Part of the difficulty lies in the way in which we immediately assume that commitment to the gospel leads to ordained ministry. It is hard for us to see beyond the clerical model to the diversity of ministries in the world. Though deeply personal, ministry is not a personal possession. The ministry is defined by Christ, and our call to ministry is an invitation to share that ministry. Often we slip carelessly into talking about "my ministry" as if we can define it as we choose. When we reduce ministry to this kind of privatism, we lose sight of the fact that Jesus' life, death, and resurrection determine the nature of ministry. At its heart, vocation is about the way God calls us to shape our humanity around a sense of calling. It is a matter of living out of a vision that comes from listening to the voice of God. The work of hearing and interpreting God's leading in our lives should be the fundamental work of ministry. The gospel tells us that our lives are a creation, and that we are, in the words of the psalmist, "fearfully and wonderfully made" (Ps. 139:14). To each of us is given the task of becoming human in the image of Jesus Christ.

This self-understanding is crucial in the way it determines how we view pastoral ministry—not as a matter of tinkering with the parts, but of discerning the sense of direction and purpose around which the congregation shapes its life. Paul wrote, "Now you are the body of Christ and individually members of it" (1 Cor. 12:27). In this context, pastoral ministry is the work of the practical theologian who is a pastor and teacher in the midst of a community of faith. This work involves helping a congregation find its way and live out the truth it is called to serve in a particular setting. This requires pastors to know the traditions of the church and to be able to communicate those traditions so that the congregation has access to the resources of faith. Most important, though, it demands that the pastor must be a human being who joins the journey of faith and sees in his or her life the diverse ways of the Word becoming incarnate. It requires that pastors must be responsible persons whose recognition of their own humanity frees them to do the work of ordained ministry to which they are called and for which they are paid.

The irony is that the less we live out of the freedom and the limits of our own humanity, the more we are prone to use the office of ministry as a means of meeting our own needs and placing demands on our congregations to make up for the deficiencies of our own lives. No congregation can provide self-esteem. No congregation can make up for the love missed as a child. No congregation can become the friend, the lover, the family so desperately sought but seldom found. Although there are voices in congregations that want to convince clergy that they are Mr. or Ms. Fix-It, we need to listen to the voices that call us to be a teacher who tells the stories of faith, a preacher who openly struggles to discern God's calling, and a leader who equips the congregation for ministry—for their priesthood and care for one another and the world.

In reflecting on the nature of ordained ministry, we need to begin with the recognition that the hardest struggle of pastoral life is not church politics, finances, or mixed-up personal relationships. Instead, the most troubling issue is the matter of the pastor's own faith. At some point, often early in ministry, a crisis comes that raises this issue, and the response to that crisis usually determines the nature of ministry ever after. Some who confront the question of their own belief recognize that they do not believe at all, that pastoral ministry is not their calling, and they leave. Others look at the gap between what they profess and who they are and find ways to construct a persona—a public mask of unending good humor and sincerity—that will allow them to play the clerical role and stay in the church's pension fund. Many, however, push away the question to the early hours of the morning. They keep their doubt in the shadows of their lives, and gradually, they impoverish their souls and the souls of all who are near them.

We live in a time in which there is a great interest in and searching for the spiritual life. Some of this search is superficial—a kind of Cook's tour of the sacred. But much of this searching is real; it is the quest to locate teachers who can make the traditions of faith available; it is the attempt to locate preachers who are credible witnesses to the truth they proclaim; and it is a life-and-death yearning for someone or someplace that points to the reality of God's presence. A member of the congregation I first served as pastor once told me, "Basically, what we want to know is what you believe, whether it makes any difference in your life, and how we can learn some things about God and our own lives in watching you." I have never forgotten those words—they have held me in wonder and terror ever since. But what permits us to live in such a "charge to ministry" is the recognition that what is important is the way we struggle with faith and continue the radical revolution of our own religious life. We cannot speak of God and the Christian life unless we seek God and try to live in Christ. We have no voice as ministers unless we have lived in the silence of prayer. Moreover, ministry is learned and practiced in the midst of the struggles that engage us. There is no spirituality, no prayer, apart from our common life. The issue is, How in the midst of our lives, in all their grittiness, do we find the fidelity that comes out of our hoping, praying, and loving—and permits us to serve God and equip the church for ministry?

SEVENTEEN

~

Renewing the Practices
of Ministry

We declare to you what was from the beginning, what we have
heard, what we have seen with our eyes, what we have looked at
and touched with our hands, concerning the word of life.

—1 John 1:1

For George MacLeod, lukewarm, conventional Presbyterianism
finally died in the Holy Land on Easter Sunday, 1933. The old
structure of individual devotion and duty had cracked in the
crucible that was Govan in the hungry thirties, and he knew in
his heart of hearts that it could not be repaired by more work,
or even by more faith. He needed, for his healing, a new way of
seeing, and he found a new vision in the midst of overwhelming,
mysteriously beautiful worship.

—Ronald Ferguson, *George MacLeod:*
Founder of the Iona Community[1]

A CONGREGATION FINDS LIFE and energy through a renewed vision of the gospel. This kind of experience led to the development of a new movement in church life—the Iona Community. In
the middle of an Orthodox Easter service, George MacLeod, a
Church of Scotland minister, was grasped by a sense of possibility
for the renewal of the church. On returning to Scotland, he formed
a community composed of workers and clergy, whose aim was to
pray and work for justice and a faithful way of being the church in
the world. The community began its work on the island of Iona on
the northwest coast of Scotland. There the workers and the clergy
restored the Benedictine abbey that had been the center of the island's
significance as a place of spiritual beauty and power.

Historically, Iona was identified with St. Columba and his missionary monks and the beginning of the church in Scotland. There a new missionary venture was launched, which continues as a community of men and women committed to worship and witness. Through its ministries of social justice, it has spoken and embodied a prophetic word; and in its worship and songs, the Iona Community has offered diverse liturgies for a renewed church. It continues to follow the classic words of George MacLeod: "I am recovering the claim that Jesus was not crucified in a cathedral between two candles, but on a cross between two thieves; on the town garbage heap; at a crossroad so cosmopolitan that they had to write his title in Hebrew and in Latin and in Greek."[2] These often quoted phrases recall the church to its mission and invite us to renew the practices of ministry.

As the church has struggled to deal with declining numbers and loss of faith, we have tried to find quick fixes and gimmicks to address theological issues. Instead of cultivating our practices of faith, which is the true meaning of church growth found in the gospel, we have defined evangelism as marketing. Instead of looking at the church's traditions of teaching and formation in faith, we have watered down our educational ministries and followed every psychological self-help movement that has come down the pike. Instead of helping the church understand worship as mystery, doxology, and mission, we have been formed by electronic images of religious entertainment that focus on making worship user-friendly and turning the minister from prophetic preacher to talk show host.

Our difficulty as a church is that, for too many of us, the Christian life is less a way of being or a set of practices than it is a range of emotions. Our images are privatistic, individualistic, and limited. We assume that the vitality of local congregations depends on our ability to sustain good feelings and to meet individual needs. The idea that there are practices of the Christian life that shape our emotions and form our commitments is a foreign understanding. The concept of faith as a discipline is not a familiar image. In this sense, the local congregation is sometimes not so much a tradition composed of practices as it is another form of entertainment that satisfies the religious feelings of spectators, who can hardly tell any difference between the dynamics of the sports arena and the church on the corner.[3] The practices of the Christian faith call us to action out of the vision that we see incarnate in the life, death, and resurrection of Jesus Christ. These practices are the practices of ministry that make up the gospel tradition. They compose the common life of the church and extend the traditions that are described in the witness of the Christian Scriptures. In Acts, for example, the community of faith is described in the following way: "They devoted themselves to the apostles' teaching and fellowship, to the breaking of bread and the prayers" (Acts 2:42).

The Christian life is expressed in proclaiming the gospel to the world and forming faithful lives within the church. It is embodied in the character of the community of faith and the nature of that community as *koinonia*, that is, communion and fellowship. These practices are sustained in worship, prayer, and the forms of spiritual life that nourish the church's mission in the world, which is the vocation of all Christians. Within this context, to think of the leadership of the church, especially the work and calling of the church's pastors and teachers, is to address the issue of renewing the ministry of the whole church. Usually, our first response to this issue of renewal is to frame it as the clerical problem of how to preach, teach, counsel, or manage. The issue is defined as how to improve these individual skills. I want to suggest, however, that these are not the practices of the ministry. These are skills and ways of knowing that may express such practices, but the practice of ministry is focused at a deeper level in three dimensions:

1. To proclaim the gospel to all the world (proclamation).
2. To build up the body of Christ (formation).
3. To equip the church for ministry (mission).

The particular way in which these practices are carried out depends upon the situation and the nature of the church's witness in any given moment. To be a pastor and teacher of the faith, a practical theologian, is to understand these practices and to help the church form its life around the mission that calls it into being; it is the calling to serve, equip, and lead the church in determining its direction in a particular place. Doing this requires knowing how to help the church appropriate the traditions of faith and form its life in the midst of conflict, competing systems, and financial realities. Second, this leadership is anchored in prayer and theological reflection. The leadership of pastors and teachers is built on a life of faith and the practice of study and contemplation. To lead the congregation in discerning its work and calling, the pastor must be a person of the Spirit. Third, leadership is centered in guiding the church as it forms its life as the body of Christ in the midst of its existence as a local culture, a voluntary association, and a religious institution. In particular, this leadership centers in how the church organizes its life, allocates its resources, and plans its outreach as a living tradition. This tradition is defined by Christ, who is the center of its witness, stewardship, and evangelism.

It is tempting in this time to feel overwhelmed by the forces of change and the continuing necessity to rethink the traditions in which we live. We are inclined to protest and whimper. When moving in that direction, I am sometimes redeemed by words that come back to me from Dietrich Bonhoeffer:

> One may ask whether there have ever before in human history been people with so little ground under their feet. . . . Or, perhaps one should rather ask whether the responsible thinking people of any generation that stood at a turning point in history did not feel as we do, simply because something new was emerging that could not be seen in the existing alternatives.[4]

We are called to live in hope, for it is a matter of faith as to what the future holds. Our questions about the church must finally be placed within the question of God's continuing revelation. We should remember that in the new heaven and new earth called into being by God, there are no religious institutions. This vision of John should make us aware that our primary concern cannot be the survival of the church as we know it. The question is how the church is called now to form its life within the promises of God that we have seen in Jesus Christ and so become a new church. This is our hope and our calling; it is the source of the renewal of the practices of the Christian life, and a way of renewing the particular practices of ordained ministry.

Notes

~

INTRODUCTION

1. My intention in using the term "liberal Protestant" is to locate the church tradition in which I have been formed and to indicate that congregations standing in this tradition, to some extent or another, are the churches I have most in mind in writing these reflections. My concern, however, is not to restore this tradition but simply to identify the context out of which I am writing. In fact, I think that any label like liberal or conservative is questionable, and certainly most suspect of all is claiming this kind of ideological and cultural perspective ahead of the gospel's claim on our lives.

While it is always difficult to use such terms and have them mean anything in particular, I think "liberal Protestant" does point to a tradition that has shaped various congregations and movements within most mainline Protestant denominations in the United States. As a theological and cultural tradition situated in various ecclesial settings and changing over time, "liberal Protestantism" has been modernist as opposed to fundamentalist in biblical interpretation, progressive in general outlook, oriented toward the social gospel, and ecumenical in ecclesial relationships. See *Between the Times: The Travail of the Protestant Establishment in America, 1900–1969*, ed. William R. Hutchison (Cambridge: Cambridge University Press, 1989). William Hutchison's essay, "Protestantism as Establishment," carefully delineates some markings of this tradition, but points out that while liberals have been identified with the Protestant establishment, the establishment has been more centrist than liberal. Also, mainline church leaders have tended to be more liberal than their constituencies that reflect a broader set of commitments; see Hutchison, 13–16.

A theological reflection on the nature of this tradition is Langdon Gilkey's essay "The Christian Congregation as Religious Community," in *American Congregations*, vol. 1, *New Perspectives in the Study of Congregations*, ed. James P. Wind and James W. Lewis (Chicago: University of Chicago Press, 1994), 100–132.

2. A lyrical memory of this era was written by Sam Keen: "I knew the topography of Judea before I could locate the Cumberland Plateau, as I knew the road

117

from Damascus to Jerusalem before I could find my way from Maryville to Knoxville. . . . I had a friend in Jesus who could walk with me in Tennessee and give me guidance, succor, and assurance" (*To a Dancing God* [New York: Harper & Row, 1970], 9). After revisiting his past, Keen moved outside the church, but the past he described is one that rings true for many. Robert W. Lynn and Elliott Wright begin their history of the Sunday school with this quote from Keen and comment: "Millions have memorized the map of the Holy Land before they could get out of home towns. The Sunday school as movement and institution has made an indelible mark on the entire cultural and educational experience of American Protestant generations" (Robert W. Lynn and Elliott Wright, *The Big Little School* [Nashville: Abingdon Press, 1980], 14).

Actually, this period of popularity obscured the deeper trends of disestablishment, which had been noticed especially in the 1920s. For this background see Robert T. Handy, *A Christian America: Protestant Hopes and Historical Realities* (New York: Oxford University Press, 1971). This fact is pointed out in the context of an analysis written by Glenn T. Miller and Robert W. Lynn, "Unexplored Territory in Congregational Studies: Cultures of Giving," an unpublished memorandum, 3 August 1995. Also, as is commonly acknowledged, church growth has been largely the result of developing new congregations and not any dramatic increase in established churches. On the other hand, most churches in the past were able to hold their own and grow enough to replenish their numbers.

3. See Tom Beaudoin, *Virtual Faith: The Irreverent Spiritual Quest of Generation X* (San Francisco: Jossey-Bass, 1998); Wade Clark Roof, *A Generation of Seekers: The Spiritual Journey of the Baby Boom Generation* (San Francisco: HarperSanFrancisco, 1993); and Robert N. Bellah, Richard Madsen, William B. Sullivan, Ann Swidler, and Steven M. Tipton, *Habits of the Heart: Individualism and Commitment in American Life* (Berkeley: University of California Press, 1985).

4. These are recurring interpretations made in the literature on the contemporary church. See Milton J. Coalter, John H. Mulder, and Louis B. Weeks, *Vital Signs: The Promise of Mainstream Protestantism* (Grand Rapids, Mich.: Eerdmans, 1996); C. Kirk Hadaway and David A. Roozen, *Rerouting the Protestant Mainstream* (Nashville: Abingdon Press, 1995); Benton Johnson, Dean R. Hoge, and Donald A. Luidens, "Mainline Churches: The Real Reason for Decline," *First Things*, no. 31 (March 1993): 13–18; and W. Clark Roof and William McKinney, *American Mainline Religion: Its Changing Shape and Future* (New Brunswick, N.J.: Rutgers University Press, 1987). For denominational implications, see Jackson W. Carroll and Wade Clark Roof, eds., *Beyond Establishment: Protestant Identity in a Post-Protestant Age* (Louisville: Westminster John Knox, 1993). New research suggests that congregational numbers have been inflated. See C. Kirk Hadaway and Penny Long Marler, "Taking Attendance," *Christian Century* 115, no. 14 (May 6, 1998): 472–75.

5. Nora Gallagher, "Things Seen and Unseen," *Doubletake* (fall 1998): 24.

6. Ibid., 24–25.

7. Ibid., 26.

8. Ibid. "Thin space" refers to the Celtic idea that there are places where God is especially close by.

9. The fundamental issue is not which form of the church is best; the issue is how the different forms of being the church can be faithful. The words of H. Richard Niebuhr sum it up: "How shall we distinguish between the church we trust and to which our loyalty under God is given and the church in which we worship, whose creeds we recite, whose educational programs we carry forward, to which we speak and sometimes in our speaking preach the gospel? . . . History and contemporary visible church life make it quite clear to us that when we say 'I believe in the Holy Catholic Church' we cannot mean this church. And yet, without it the community of faith does not exist, anymore than the personal self which lives by faith exists without mind and without body" (H. Richard Niebuhr, *Faith on Earth: An Inquiry into the Structure of Human Faith*, ed. Richard R. Niebuhr [New Haven, Conn.: Yale University Press, 1989], 117–18).

10. Robert Grudin, *The Grace of Great Things: Creativity and Innovation* (New York: Ticknor & Fields, 1990), 242.

11. Ibid., 243.

12. Douglas R. A. Hare, *Matthew* (Louisville: John Knox, 1993), 126–30.

13. Also see Joseph A. Fitzmyer's discussion of the "on the road" theme in his two-volume commentary, *The Gospel According to Luke*, Anchor Bible, vols. 28, 28a (Garden City, N.Y.: Doubleday, 1985), 28:169. Also, I have assumed his interpretation of the Emmaus road event in this discussion; see 28a:1553–69.

14. Jan Wojcik, *The Road to Emmaus: Reading Luke's Gospel* (West Lafayette, Ind.: Purdue University Press, 1989), see especially 17–19, 105–41.

15. T. S. Eliot, "Little Gidding," in *Four Quartets* (New York: Harcourt Brace Jovanovich, 1971), 55.

16. This phrase is used in early liturgies of the Iona Community.

17. Walker Percy, *The Message in the Bottle* (New York: Farrar, Straus & Giroux, 1975), 144.

18. Paul Hanson, *The People Called: The Growth of Community in the Bible* (San Francisco: Harper & Row, 1986), 518.

PART 1: DESCRIBING THE PRESENT

1. Northrop Frye, *Creation and Recreation* (Toronto: University of Toronto Press, 1980), 25.

1. THE PERSISTENCE OF EXILE

1. Andrei Codrescu, *The Disappearance of the Outside* (Reading, Mass.: Addison-Wesley, 1990), 54.

2. See Iris Murdoch, *Metaphysics as a Guide to Morals* (London: Penguin Books, 1992), 7. She writes: "Metaphysical problems now reach the popular consciousness in the form of a sense of loss, of being returned to a confused pluralistic world from which something 'deep' has been removed."

3. *Semrad: The Heart of a Therapist*, ed. Susan Rako and Harvey Mazer (Northvale, N.J.: Jason Aronson, 1983), 45.

4. Tim O'Brien, *The Things They Carried* (New York: Penguin Books, 1990), 4.

5. Ibid., 20. On this theme, Paul S. Minear writes: "Each day, the pilgrim must ask again: what am I able to take along? what must I take? So whenever we think of ourselves as pilgrims, we begin instinctively to choose and to reject, to weigh and to measure, whatever is to go with us" (*To Die and to Live: Christ's Resurrection and Christian Vocation* [New York: Seabury Press, 1977], 4).

6. In this discussion of Ezekiel 12:1–20, the commentaries I have consulted include Walther Eichrodt, *Ezekiel* (Philadelphia: Westminster Press, 1970), 146–58, and Ronald E. Clements, *Ezekiel* (Louisville: Westminster John Knox, 1996), 51–61.

7. As Clements suggests, "Once again the prophet conveys the message through his preferred medium of street theater, the carefully enacted sign action that will illustrate through silent mime his ominous forewarning" (*Ezekiel*, 53).

8. In *Israel in Exile: A Theological Interpretation* (Philadelphia: Fortress Press, 1979), Ralph W. Klein writes: "Exile is a time for hope, not triumphalism. . . . To say only no to exile is triumphalism; to say only yes is hopelessness. To say yes and no is to affirm the judgment, to recognize this exilic existence as our real vocation, and yet to confess and actualize the transforming power of the Promiser" (151).

9. Mary Caroline Richards, *The Public School and the Education of the Whole Person* (New York: The Pilgrim Press, 1980), 9.

2. MEMORY AND PROMISE

1. Carlyle Marney, quoted in *Marney*, ed. Mary Kratt (Charlotte, N.C.: Myers Park Baptist Church, 1979), 92.

2. John Updike, *Hugging the Shore* (New York: Knopf, 1983), 65–66.

3. Ibid., 67.

4. See John Updike, *Museums and Women* (New York: Fawcett World Library, 1973), 16.

5. Jane Hamilton, interview with Art Jester, *Lexington Herald-Leader* (Lexington, Ky.), March 29, 1998, J-2. For another view, see the essays by Anthony B. Robinson

and Martin B. Copenhaver, "The Making of a Postliberal: Two Stories," *Christian Century* 115 (October 14, 1998): Robinson's "Beyond Civic Faith," 933–36, and Copenhaver's "Formed and Reformed," 933, 937–40.

6. Jane Hamilton, *A Map of the World* (New York: Doubleday, 1994), 301. Also, I want to thank my colleague, Jane McAvoy, for reminding me of this novel, and Pam Warford for many conversations about its meaning.

7. Ibid.

8. Ibid., 388.

9. Ibid., 26.

10. Ibid., 40.

11. Ibid.

12. Ibid., 30.

3. PILGRIMS AND TOURISTS

1. Daniel J. Boorstin, *Hidden History* (New York: Vintage Books, 1989), 302.

2. Anne Tyler, *The Accidental Tourist* (New York: Knopf, 1985), 12.

3. Ibid.

4. See Margaret Miles, "Pilgrimage as Metaphor in a Nuclear Age," *Theology Today* 45 (1988): 166–69.

5. Richard R. Niebuhr, "Pilgrims and Pioneers," *Parabola* 9, no. 3 (1984): 12. In thinking about the nature of pilgrimage in its social and cultural meanings, I have appreciated James Clifford's collection of essays on travel: James Clifford, *Routes: Travel and Translation in the Late Twentieth Century* (Cambridge: Harvard University Press, 1997). On the connection between pilgrimage and spirituality, I recommend Philip Sheldrake's *Living Between Worlds: Places and Journey in Celtic Spirituality* (London: Darton, Longman, Todd, 1995).

6. Helmut Koester, "'Outside the Camp': Hebrews 13.9–14," *Harvard Theological Review* 55 (1962): 302–15.

7. Ibid., 302.

PART 2: RELEARNING THE GOSPEL

1. Søren Kierkegaard, *Training in Christianity*, trans. with intro. and notes by Walter Lowrie (Princeton, N.J.: Princeton University Press, 1946), 281.

4. *METANOIA*: A WAY OF THINKING

1. Eugen Rosenstock-Huessy, *I Am an Impure Thinker* (Norwich, Vt.: Argo Books, 1970), 189.

2. Søren Kierkegaard, "Armed Neutrality," in *Armed Neutrality and an Open Letter*, ed. and trans. Howard V. Hong and Edna H. Hong (Bloomington: Indiana University Press, 1968), 35.

3. Percy, *The Message in the Bottle*, 3.

4. Ibid., 7.

5. Like many others, H. Richard Niebuhr makes this point, in *The Meaning of Revelation* (New York: Macmillan, 1941), 36.

6. Ibid., 80-86, 139.

7. I am following Walker Percy's discussion of Helen Keller, in *The Message in the Bottle*, 34-42.

8. Helen Keller, *The Story of My Life* (Garden City, N.Y.: Doubleday, Page and Company, 1927), 23-24. Also, Anne Sullivan's reflections on the event, 315-16.

9. Ibid., 24.

10. Karl Barth, *The Epistle to the Romans*, translated from the sixth edition by Edwyn C. Hoskyns (London: Oxford University Press, 1963), 386.

11. Ibid., 425.

12. Ibid.

13. Ibid., 434-35.

14. Rosenstock-Huessy, *I Am an Impure Thinker*, 189.

15. For an extended discussion of conversion, see Beverly Roberts Gaventa, *From Darkness to Light: Aspects of Conversion in the New Testament* (Philadelphia: Fortress, 1986).

5. HEARING AND SEEING

1. Flannery O'Connor, "The Fiction Writer and His Country," in *Collected Works*, ed. Sally Fitzgerald (New York: Library of America, 1988), 805-6.

2. The commentaries I have consulted in interpreting the story of Nicodemus and Jesus' meeting with the Samaritan woman are Raymond E. Brown, *The Gospel According to John I-XII*, Anchor Bible (New York: Doubleday, 1966), and George R. Beasley-Murray, *John*, Word Biblical Commentary (Waco, Tex.: Word, 1987). Also, see Larry Paul Jones, "The Symbol of Water in the Gospel of John," *Journal for the Study of the New Testament*, n.s. 145 (Sheffield, Eng.: Sheffield Academic Press, 1997), 65-114.

3. William Stafford, "The Gift," in *My Name Is William Tell* (Lewiston, Idaho: Confluence, 1992), 49.

4. For several years, Tom Carson and Paul Peters led congregations across the United States in developing ways of listening to one another and the communities in which they were located. This was a project of the UCC Board for Homeland Ministries.

6. WISDOM AND FOLLY

1. Quoted in *Thy Kingdom Come: A Blumhardt Reader*, ed. Vernard Eller (Grand Rapids, Mich.: Eerdmans, 1980), frontispiece.

2. For an extended discussion of this kind of listening and learning, see Eudora Welty, *One Writer's Beginnings* (Cambridge: Harvard University Press, 1983). The divisions of this autobiography are "listening," "learning to see," and "finding a voice." Welty's description of adults prompted my own memories of similar moments.

3. See Robert Coles's account of the story of Ruby in *Harvard Diary* (New York: Crossroad, 1988), 134–41, and in the video *Robert Coles: An Intimate Biographical Interview*, ed. Bruce Baird-Middletown, 60 min. (Cambridge: Harvard University Press, n.d.).

4. Robert Coles, *The Story of Ruby Bridges* (New York: Scholastic, 1995).

5. See Flannery O'Connor, *The Habit of Being*, letters edited by Sally Fitzgerald (New York: Farrar, Straus & Giroux, 1979).

6. Coles, *Harvard Diary*, 135–36.

7. Robert Coles, "Ruby," in *Rumors of Separate Worlds* (Iowa City: University of Iowa Press, 1989), 33.

8. Charles Lemert, *Social Things* (Lanham, Md.: Rowman & Littlefield, 1997), 190.

7. A NEW BELONGING

1. Kurt Lewin, quoted in C. Ellis Nelson, *Where Faith Begins* (Atlanta: John Knox Press, 1967), 102.

2. *The Heidelberg Catechism*, ed. and trans. Allen O. Miller and M. Eugene Osterhaven (Philadelphia: United Church Press, 1962), 9. I am grateful to Professor Allen Miller for introducing me to this text and to C. Ellis Nelson for ways of understanding the dynamics of belonging to the Christian community that lie at the heart of *Where Faith Begins*. The notion of belonging took on new meaning for me in reading Br. Leonard of Taizé, *Belonging* (New York: The Pilgrim Press, 1985). Craig Dykstra thoughtfully discusses issues of faith and knowing in *Growing in the Life of Faith: Education and Christian Practices* (Louisville: Geneva Press, 1999), 17–49. The philosopher Alasdair MacIntyre draws a connection between belonging and the narratives that claim us: "I can only answer the question 'What am I to do?' if I can answer the prior question 'Of what story or stories do I find myself a part?'" See *After Virtue* (Notre Dame, Ind.: University of Notre Dame Press, 1984), 216.

3. Walker Percy, *The Second Coming* (New York: Farrar, Straus & Giroux, 1980), 93. One of the novel's characters states, "I made straight A's and flunked ordinary living."

4. Rainer Maria Rilke, *Rilke on Love and Other Difficulties*, ed. John J. L. Mood (New York: W. W. Norton, 1975), 31.

5. Tracy Kidder, *Among Schoolchildren* (Boston: Houghton Mifflin, 1989), 313.

6. Hans Hoekendijk Jr., *Horizons of Hope* (Nashville: Tidings, 1970), 36. Also, see Peter L. Berger, *A Rumor of Angels* (Garden City, N.Y.: Doubleday, 1969), 120, where this quote from the French worker priests is translated: "So that the rumor of God may not disappear completely."

7. Percy, *The Second Coming*, 123–24.

8. Ibid., 124.

8. VOCATION: THE HOPE OF OUR CALLING

1. Hans-Ruedi Weber, *Living in the Image of Christ* (Geneva: WCC Publications, 1986), 12.

2. James Agee and Walker Evans, *Let Us Now Praise Famous Men* (Boston: Houghton Mifflin, 1941), 289. Or as James M. Gustafson writes: "My strong hunch is that to be human is to have a vocation, a calling; that it is to become what we now are not; that it calls for a surpassing of what we are; that apart from a *telos*, a vision of what man can and ought to do, we will flounder and decay" (*Theology and Christian Ethics* [Philadelphia: United Church Press, 1974], 244). Quoted in Paul S. Minear, *To Die and to Live*, 23.

3. Agee and Evans, *Let Us Now Praise Famous Men*, 289.

4. Dag Hammarskjöld, *Markings*, trans. Leif Sjöberg and W. H. Auden (New York: Knopf, 1964), 205.

5. These are the questions found on a painting of a Polynesian scene by Paul Gaugin (1897). David Hackett Fischer observes, "The canvas is crowded with brooding figures in every condition of life—young and old, dark and fair. They are seen in a forest of symbols as if part of a dream. In the corner, the artist has added an inscription: '*D'ou venons nous? Qui sommes nous? Ou allons nous?*'" (David Hackett Fischer, *Albion's Seed: Four British Folkways in America* [New York: Oxford University Press, 1989], 3). Also, see the video *Robert Coles: An Intimate Biographical Interview*.

6. Eugen Rosenstock-Huessy, *The Christian Future or the Modern Mind Outrun* (New York: Charles Scribner's Sons, 1946), 94.

7. Quoted in Robert Coles, *Privileged Ones*, vol. 5 of *Children of Crisis* (Boston: Little, Brown, 1977), 552–53.

8. Welty, *One Writer's Beginnings*, 68–69.

9. Mary Catherine Bateson, *Composing a Life* (New York: Atlantic Monthly Press, 1985), 3.

10. Ibid., 15.

11. Jesse Stuart, *The Thread That Runs So True* (New York: Scribner's, 1949).

12. Dietrich Bonhoeffer, *Christology*, trans. John Bowden (New York: Harper & Row, 1966), 61.

13. Ibid., 61–62.

14. James Still, *River of Earth* (Lexington: University Press of Kentucky, 1978), 76.

15. James M. Gustafson's essay "Professions as 'Callings'" is a critical examination of the idea of calling. Gustafson looks at traditional Calvinist and Lutheran understandings of calling, discusses both their transforming and their controlling aspects, and offers a contemporary view of the relationship between calling and professionalization (*Social Service Review* [December 1982]: 501–15).

16. In this discussion of biblical meanings of vocation, I am indebted to the work of Paul S. Minear, who sets the idea of calling within the shared vocation of the community of faith. See *To Die and to Live* and "Work and Vocation in Scripture," in *Work and Vocation*, ed. John Oliver Nelson (New York: Harper's, 1954), 35–81.

17. Minear, *Work and Vocation*, 53.

18. Ibid.

19. Ibid.

20. Frederick Buechner, *The Sacred Journey* (San Francisco: Harper & Row, 1982), 77–78.

PART 3: PRACTICES OF FAITH

1. Elizabeth Hardwick, *Sleepless Nights* (London: Virago, 1986), 14.

9. THE CHURCH'S WITNESS

1. Emmanuel, Cardinal Suhard, "The Priest in the Modern World," in *The Pastoral Letters of Emmanuel, Cardinal Suhard* (London: New Life, 1955), 153.

2. Flannery O'Connor, *Collected Works*, 478. Quoted in Margaret Earley Whitt, *Understanding Flannery O'Connor* (Columbia: University of South Carolina Press, 1995), 2. In *Flannery O'Connor and Cold War Culture* (Cambridge: Cambridge University Press, 1993), Jon Lance Bacon points out that O'Connor speaks of "an 'invisible country' of the faithful," which I have referred to in this paragraph as the "country of faith." See Bacon, 136.

3. See Clifford Geertz, "The Uses of Diversity," *Michigan Quarterly Review* 25, no. 1 (winter 1986): 105–23, and Richard Rorty, "On Ethnocentrism: A Reply to Clifford Geertz," *Michigan Quarterly Review* 25, no. 3 (summer 1986): 525–34. The exchange between Geertz and Rorty focuses on the nature of contemporary culture as a "bazaar."

4. One extant model is that of the church as "colony." While I am reluctant to use the imagery of "colony" because of the way in which this term tends toward an uncritical separation from the society in which the church exists, Stanley Hauerwas and William H. Willimon struggle with such issues in their effort to appropriate this kind of imagery in *Resident Aliens* (Nashville: Abingdon, 1993). An earlier use of the colony imagery is found in George W. Webber, *God's Colony in Man's World* (Nashville: Abingdon, 1960), which is the story of the East Harlem Protestant Parish.

5. John Calvin, *Calvin: Institutes of the Christian Religion*, vol. 1, ed. John T. McNeill, trans. Ford L. Battles (Philadelphia: Westminster Press, 1960), 6.1, 70.

6. James Agee, *The Collected Poems of James Agee* (Boston: Houghton Mifflin, 1968), 15.

7. On the nature of theological diversity in the church, see Michael Kinnamon's essay "Pluralism and Church-Related Higher Education," where he affirms that "unity (wholeness) and diversity (particularity) must be held in dialectical tension in any theologically acceptable understanding of the church and the faith it confesses. An emphasis on unity that does not value human diversity, including diversity of perspective, easily becomes bland and authoritarian; but an emphasis on diversity without concern for what Paul calls 'the common good' easily becomes fragmented and provincial" ([Cleveland: United Church Board for Homeland Ministries, 1996], 5–6).

8. Two recent books that deal with diversity and inclusiveness in the church are Charles R. Foster and Theodore Brelsford, *We Are the Church Together: Cultural Diversity in Congregational Life* (Valley Forge, Pa.: Trinity Press International, 1996), and David Rhoads, *The Challenge of Diversity: The Witness of Paul and the Gospels* (Minneapolis: Augsburg, 1996).

10. THE CHURCH'S WORSHIP

1. Neil Postman, *Amusing Ourselves to Death* (New York: Penguin Books, 1986), 124.

2. C. S. Lewis, *The Screwtape Letters* (London: Geoffrey Bles, 1961), 26. Also, Edward Farley makes the point: "The casual, happy, amused and chatty Sunday morning has crept upon us unawares." He wonders that if this kind of gathering is going to be around for a while, "perhaps congregations face the difficult task of creating another time or event in their ritual life when people gather to adore." See Edward Farley, "A Missing Presence," *Christian Century* 115 (March 18–25, 1998): 277. In this regard, worship has become many different things, not just praise and thanksgiving to God. We have collapsed several church gatherings into this time on Sunday morning with the result that worship takes on characteristics once assigned to the

Sunday school assembly, the Wednesday evening prayer meeting, the missionary society, and weekend fellowship party. In a way, all of these are elements of worship, but without any sense of ordering and understanding these various expectations collapse under their own weight as competing interests rather than dimensions of the praise of God. One step toward addressing this concern is to look again at what we intend to do in any gathering of the church, and especially what we intend in worship.

3. See Marshall McLuhan's discussion of these issues in *The Medium and the Light: Reflections on Religion*, ed. Eric McLuhan and Jacek Szklarek (Toronto: Stoddart Publishing Company, 1999), especially "International Motley and Religious Costume," 75–79.

4. See Ernest Albrecht, *The New American Circus* (Gainesville: University Press of Florida, 1995). The new American circuses include the Big Apple Circus, Cirque du Soleil, Circus Flora, and earlier projects like the Pickle Family Circus. In tracing the history of these circuses, Albrecht points out that most of them sought to make connections between an artistic vision and involvement in social issues. In describing the three-ring circuses, he depicts how various circuses persisted in the three-ring, spectacle model even when they had neither the finances nor the talent to pursue it. In words that could equally describe many congregations, he writes, "Even the most woebegone of truck shows spread their wares, however sparse, over three circular arenas"(2).

5. Ibid., 66–96.

6. See Jonathan Edwards, *Religious Affections*, ed. John E. Smith, *The Works of Jonathan Edwards*, vol. 2, ed. Perry Miller (New Haven, Conn.: Yale University Press, 1959), 253–59, 271–75. Edwards speaks of the "supreme beauty and excellency of the nature of divine things, as they are in themselves" (271).

7. See T. S. Eliot, "The Social Function of Poetry," in *On Poetry and Poets* (London: Faber & Faber, 1957), 19. Also see Wendell Berry, *The Work of Local Culture* (Iowa City: Iowa Humanities Board, 1988).

8. Eliot, "The Social Function of Poetry," 24.

9. The church was Highlands Congregational Church, UCC, in Melrose, Massachusetts, and the minister was Charles Barnes.

11. STEWARDS

1. Gary Snyder, *The Practice of the Wild* (San Francisco: North Point Press, 1990), 21.

2. Obviously, this is not the donor's actual name.

3. Quoted in Robert Wuthnow, *The Crisis in the Churches: Spiritual Malaise, Fiscal Woe* (New York: Oxford University Press, 1997), 14.

4. Ibid., 242. Also 68–70.

5. This is a summary of Wuthnow's discussion; see especially 238–40.

6. Ibid., 223.

7. Ibid., 223–24.

8. In a similar way, Kirk Hadaway and David Roozen affirm: "We argue that the route to vitality is emergent in the increasing number of mainstream congregations that have their grounding in spiritually oriented worship, contagious with the expectation, the presumption, the surety that God is present and active" (*Rerouting the Protestant Mainstream*, 129). This is a clear and helpful book on church growth and change. It does not hold back from the difficult news, but it provides a way of interpreting the present moment that is faithful to the liberal Protestant tradition, essentially recalling this tradition to its fundamental commitments.

9. Dietrich Bonhoeffer, *Ethics*, ed. Eberhard Bethge, trans. Neville Horton Smith (New York: Macmillan, 1955), 258. I was reminded of this passage by reading Richard R. Broholm's essay, "How Can You Believe You're a Minister When the Church Keeps Telling You You're Not?" in *The Laity in Ministry*, ed. George Peck and John S. Hoffman (Valley Forge, Pa.: Judson, 1984), 24.

10. Wendell Berry, *What Are People For?* (San Francisco: North Point, 1990), 96–97.

11. Ibid.

12. *The Book of Common Prayer* (New York: Seabury, 1928), 44.

13. *The Book of Common Prayer* (New York: Seabury, 1977), 210.

14. Berry, *What Are People For?*,101.

15. Hans-Ruedi Weber, *The Militant Ministry: People and Pastors of the Early Church and Today* (Philadelphia: Fortress, 1963), 57–58.

16. Gregory Bateson, "The Oak Beams of New College, Oxford," in *The Next Whole Earth Catalog*, ed. Stewart Brand (New York: Random House, 1980), 77. I first found this story in 1980 when I was at Union and working with the strategic planning committee. Bateson's story was the introduction to what became known as "The Wilson Report." The story seemed appropriate then and now as a reminder of our long-term commitments in institutional life.

12. GENEROSITY OF SPIRIT

1. Wendell Berry, *Recollected Essays 1965–1989* (San Francisco: North Point, 1981), 210.

13. LARGE THINGS IN A SMALL PARISH

1. Paul Moore, *Presences: A Bishop's Life in the City* (New York: Farrar, Straus & Giroux, 1997), 314.

2. Kim Klein, *Being the Church in Columbia Heights*, ed. Gerald Fitzgerald and William R. MacKaye (privately published, 1992), 13.

3. R. S. Thomas, *The Echoes Return Slow* (London: Macmillan, 1988), 25.

4. In thinking about the questions of congregational vocation, I have benefited from Douglas F. Ottati's *Reforming Protestantism: Christian Commitment in Today's World* (Louisville: Westminster John Knox, 1995). This has been especially so in reflecting on the nature of the church as both *ekklesia* and *koinonia*; see 93–116. At the heart of his understanding of a "reforming Protestantism" is the calling to "the sanctification of the ordinary and mundane disciplining of the spiritual" (137).

14. COMMUNION

1. Donald Hall, "The Art of Poetry XLIII," *Paris Review*, no. 120 (fall 1991): 190.

2. Donald Hall, *Here at Eagle Pond* (New York: Ticknor & Fields, 1990), 4–5.

3. Ibid., 5.

4. Donald Hall and Jane Kenyon, "A Journey from Community to Communion," *Horizons*, no. 1 (spring 1995): 18.

5. Ibid.

6. Ibid., 42–43.

7. Ibid., 18.

8. Ibid.

9. Ibid., 43.

10. Jane Kenyon, "Having It Out with Melancholy," *Otherwise: New and Selected Poems* (St. Paul, Minn.: Graywolf, 1996), 192.

11. Jane Kenyon, "Peonies at Dusk," in *Otherwise*, 207.

12. Jane Kenyon, "Looking at Stars," in *Otherwise*, 175.

13. Jane Kenyon, "Let Evening Come," in *Otherwise*, 176.

14. Donald Hall, "Weeds and Peonies," in *Without* (New York: Houghton Mifflin, 1998), 81.

15. Donald Hall, "Letter after a Year," in *Without*, 77–78.

16. Jane Kenyon, "Notes from the Other Side," in *Otherwise*, 215.

PART 4: SERVING AND LEADING

1. Susan Kenney, *Sailing* (New York: Viking, 1988), 16.

15. LEADERS DEEP DOWN INSIDE

1. Robert K. Greenleaf, *The Servant as Religious Leader* (Indianapolis: Robert K. Greenleaf Center, 1982), 7.

2. Robert K. Greenleaf, *Servant Leadership: A Journey into the Nature of Legitimate Power and Greatness* (New York: Paulist, 1977).

3. Robert K. Greenleaf, *The Servant as Leader* (Peterborough, N.H.: Center for Applied Studies, 1970), 8.

4. Ibid., 7–8.

5. Robert K. Greenleaf, "*Entheos* and Growth," in *On Becoming a Servant Leader*, ed. Don M. Frick and Larry C. Spears (San Francisco: Jossey-Bass, 1996), 82.

6. Max De Pree says succinctly: "The first responsibility of a leader is to define reality. The last is to say thank you. In between the two, the leader must become a servant and a debtor. That sums up the process of an artful leader" (*Leadership Is an Art* [New York: Doubleday, 1989], 9).

7. Greenleaf, *The Servant as Leader*, 14–19.

8. Wendell Berry, *A Continuous Harmony* (New York: Harcourt Brace Jovanovich, 1972), 135.

9. Greenleaf, *The Servant as Leader*, 14–16.

10. See Ronald A. Heifetz, *Leadership without Easy Answers* (Cambridge: Harvard University Press, 1994), 250.

11. Greenleaf, *The Servant as Leader*, 2.

16. THE SILENCE OF PRAYER AND THE VOICE OF MINISTRY

1. Max Picard, *The World of Silence*, trans. Stanley Godman (Chicago: Henry Regnery, 1952), 228.

2. See H. Richard Niebuhr, *The Purpose of the Church and Its Ministry* (New York: Harper & Row, 1956), 64–65. This discussion of calling is based on Niebuhr's analysis.

3. See Taylor Branch, *Parting the Waters: America in the King Years, 1954–63* (New York: Simon & Schuster, 1988), 106–205.

4. Stephen B. Oates, *Let the Trumpet Sound* (New York: Harper & Row, 1982), 88–89.

5. See the essay on ordination written by the faculty of Eden Theological Seminary, "Perspective on Ordination" (St. Louis: Eden Seminary, 1983).

6. The World Council of Churches' statement on baptism, eucharist, and ministry goes on to affirm: "Ordained ministers can fulfill their calling only and for the community. They cannot dispense with the recognition, the support, and the encouragement of the community" ("Baptism, Eucharist, and Ministry," *Faith and Order Paper No. 111* [Geneva: WCC Publications, 1982], 22).

17. RENEWING THE PRACTICES OF MINISTRY

1. Ronald Ferguson, *George MacLeod: Founder of the Iona Community* (London: William Collins Sons, 1990), 110.

2. George F. MacLeod, *Only One Way Left* (Glasgow: Iona Community, 1958), 38.

3. The term "practice" is used here in the sense described by Alasdair MacIntyre in *After Virtue* as "any coherent and complex form of socially established cooperative human activity through which goods internal to that form of activity are realized in the course of trying to achieve those standards of excellence which are appropriate to, and partially definitive of, that form of activity, with the result that human powers to achieve excellence, and human conceptions of the ends and goods involved, are systematically extended" (187). The term is clarified by Robert Bellah et al. in *Habits of the Heart*: "Practices are shared activities that are not undertaken as a means to an end but are ethically good in themselves. . . . A genuine community—whether a marriage, a university, or a whole society—is constituted by such practices" (334). Craig Dykstra situates the idea of practice within the Christian community in "Reconceiving Practice," in *Shifting Boundaries*, ed. Barbara G. Wheeler and Edward Farley (Louisville: Westminster/John Knox, 1991), 35–66. In *Growing in Faith*, he defines practices as "patterns of communal action that create openings in our lives where the grace, mercy, and presence of God may be known to us. . . . In the end, these are not ultimately our practices but forms of participation in the practice of God" (66). For diverse expressions of practices see Dorothy Bass, ed., *Practicing Our Faith: A Way of Life for a Searching People* (San Francisco: Jossey-Bass, 1997).

4. Dietrich Bonhoeffer, *Letters and Papers from Prison*, ed. Eberhard Bethge, trans. Reginald H. Fuller (New York: Macmillan, 1953), 16.

Colloquy

Questions for Conversation

~

Introduction

1. What do the images of weary pilgrims and occasional tourists suggest for you?
2. Are there signs of weariness in your congregation? What are the places of joy?
3. What does the term "liberal Protestant" mean to you? Would you identify yourself in this way?
4. Does the organizational structure of your congregation seem out of sorts with your hopes for the church? If so, what needs to be changed?
5. How does the story of Jesus with the disciples on the road to Emmaus help you interpret this moment in the life of your church?

PART 1: DESCRIBING THE PRESENT

1. The Persistence of Exile

1. How do you experience the church as being in exile? What does this image convey to you when thinking about the life of your congregation? As the church has lost its established place in society, what do we need to understand about this time? How does the biblical story of Exile inform this present moment?
2. What is your sadness about the church? If sadness is related to not getting what we want, what is it that you want the church to be? What are the questions that are most important to you and to your congregation?

3. If you, like Ezekiel, had to choose just a few things to take with you to a new future for the church, what would they be? What would you leave behind?

4. How does the church's experience of exile broaden your understanding of what exile means for displaced peoples throughout the world?

5. What is your congregation called now to be and to do? How is this different from or the same as what its ministries have been in the past?

2. Memory and Promise

1. Does your church sometimes feel like a museum? What creates this feeling?

2. What are the elements of faith that are the substance of the church? What do you think of Jane Hamilton's comment that her religious upbringing gave her "Wonder Bread" rather than substantive faith?

3. What do you look for in your life? What are the sources of meaning for you? Do you find this meaning in the church? If not, where do you find, or where are you found by, this sense of purpose and meaning? How does God speak to you?

4. What does the church need to reclaim in its life? What has been lost or forgotten along the way?

3. Pilgrims and Tourists

1. What is the difference between being a tourist and being a pilgrim in your life and the life of the church?

2. What does it mean to describe life as a pilgrimage?

3. Do you experience the church as a place or as a movement?

4. What have been places of turning in your life?

5. Jesus seems to say that home is not just a destination, but it is also a journey. What has happened to you on the road? In traveling have you found yourself to be a pilgrim and not just a tourist?

PART 2: RELEARNING THE GOSPEL

4. Metanoia: *A Way of Thinking*

1. What does it mean to you to be called a Christian?
2. Where do you learn about faith? How do you share this faith with others?
3. Have you experienced moments of transformation—the kind of learning in which your thinking has been changed and your life formed in a different way?
4. What images come to mind when you think of the word "repentance"? What are the dimensions of repentance in your life? What have you known of forgiveness and grace?
5. Have you ever been "unwilling to continue" with the way things are in your life or in the life of the church?

5. Hearing and Seeing

1. What do you see as the differences between the Samaritan woman and Nicodemus? How do these stories help interpret your own struggle with faith?
2. Have you ever had a sense of the "other country" that William Stafford speaks of in the poem in this chapter?
3. What questions haunt you or keep returning to your heart and mind?
4. How does the gospel speak to these questions?

6. Wisdom and Folly

1. What stories have claimed your life in a special way? What stories do you remember from childhood that have shaped you in some way?
2. What stories do you tell to others to give them some sense of who you are and what is important to you?
3. Where do you hear the stories of others? Have there been key stories told by others that have changed you in any way?

4. Ruby Bridges grew up in a church that gave her stories which shaped her life and gave her a way of responding in a crucial moment. How is your church such a community of faith? How could it become more like this kind of community?

7. A New Belonging

1. Where do you belong? Who claims you and what are you claimed by?
2. What are the important places of belonging in your life? In your family, neighborhood, work, country, race, class?
3. How do you discern the world in which you live? What do you take for granted as being real? How does the gospel invite you to rethink these assumptions about the world?
4. What do you think of Tracy Kidder's description of people who do good without taking credit? Do you know such people?
5. Have you ever had the feeling of "missing your life"? How did you find your way again? Have you had the experience of being found by God?

8. Vocation: The Hope of Our Calling

1. What is your calling in life? Who or what is it that calls you? How does God call you?
2. What is the relationship between your calling and the work you do? How has your sense of calling changed over time?
3. What biblical stories help you understand the nature of calling?
4. What does it mean for Christ to "stand for us"—between the old and new self we struggle to become?

PART 3: PRACTICES OF FAITH

9. The Church's Witness

1. How is the church called to be different from other voluntary associations?
2. How would that difference inform how the church allocates its resources and what it does in the world?
3. What does it mean for the church to be inclusive?

4. Are there normative elements of faith that establish a center for the church's life? Are there times in which being inclusive sometimes seems to suggest that nothing really matters? How then do we decide what we have to hold to and what we need to hold more lightly?
5. How is Christ the center of your congregation's life? What statements of belief or affirmations of faith are essential to being part of the church?
6. How does the church invite and gather others into its community? What are forms of hospitality the church should practice?

10. The Church's Worship

1. What do you expect in worship? What do you find in the worship of your congregation? Is it an occasion of praise and thanksgiving to God?
2. Does the church sometimes feel like a three-ring circus? Describe some occasions when this has been most apparent in your church's worship.
3. How would you begin to think about the renewal of worship in the life of the congregation?
4. What are moments in the church's worship when you have seen the connection between liturgy and the life of the world? What brought about these moments when worship ceased being entertainment and became the work of the people of God?

11. Stewards

1. How do you make decisions about money? Where and with whom do you feel free to discuss financial issues in your life?
2. How do you make decisions about your time and the use of your gifts? Would you want to change anything about your use of time and your gifts?
3. Do you think the church has become too activity centered? How would you change the church's programs and commitments to be more faithful to the gospel?
4. What meaning does stewardship have for you?

12. *Generosity of Spirit*

1. Do you think that faith sometimes requires us to "put all our eggs in one basket"?
2. Do you have stories of generosity of spirit? What effect have these stories had on your life?
3. How does change occur in the church? Have you seen real change take place?
4. What do you think holds us back from renewing the church?

13. *Large Things in a Small Parish*

1. What ministries are needed to equip the church for its mission in the world? What is the particular work of pastors, the ministries of elders, deacons, and/or other authorized offices of leadership in the church?
2. How could your church function without the model of full-time professional clergy? How would it change the life of the congregation? How would you discern leaders in your midst? How would they be prepared and authorized for ministry?
3. In a church with a full-time pastor, to what extent do you think the pastor is primarily expected to minister to the congregation rather than equip the congregation for its ministry in life and work?
4. What old forms need to be dismantled in your congregation or what forgotten forms should be brought back? What new structures does the church need in order to renew its ministry and mission?

14. *Communion*

1. What is the relationship between community and communion?
2. What is the relationship between belonging and believing?
3. Who has shaped your understanding of the gospel? Where were you taught and formed in faith? Describe some of the persons who were your teachers in faith.

4. How has God transformed your life? Where did this journey in faith begin? How did it change along the way? What are the questions of faith in your life now?

PART 4: SERVING AND LEADING

15. Leaders Deep Down Inside

1. Who are the leaders you admire? Why?
2. How do you find leaders? How do you know how well they are leading?
3. Compare and contrast the leadership images of cheerleader, teacher, and manager.
4. How is leadership spiritual work?
5. Who are the servant-leaders you have seen?

16. The Silence of Prayer and the Voice of Ministry

1. What does it mean to speak of yourself as a minister of the gospel?
2. How are you called into that ministry? What are the particular gifts that you have to offer for ministry? How have you found ways of expressing these gifts?
3. Who are your companions in discussing these questions?
4. What is the relationship between Christ's ministry and our own?
5. What are the practices of prayer and contemplation that undergird your life in faith? Do you find it difficult to pray? Why? How could you learn to pray?

17. Renewing the Practices of Ministry

1. Is there a future for the form of the church we have known as liberal Protestantism? Is it useful any longer even to use such terms as liberal or conservative?
2. What are the essential practices of the church? Describe how some of these are carried out in congregational life.

3. Where do you look for signs of God's call to renew the church?
4. If your congregation experienced a season of renewal, how would it be transformed? What would be reclaimed? What would the church no longer do, do differently, or begin to do?
5. What are your hopes for becoming a new church?

Index

~

Abbey of Gethsemani, 101
Accidental Tourist, The (Tyler), 22
adolescents, 45, 94. *See also* children
Agee, James, 53
Albrecht, Ernest, 68
American Baptist Church, 79, 117 n. 1
associations and clubs, 62, 64, 73–74
attendance, church. *See* church
    membership

Babylonian exile, 10. *See also* Ezekiel
    (prophet)
baggage, in exile, 10–14
Bangor Seminary, 89
baptism, 52, 53, 105
Barth, Karl, 34–35
Bateson, Gregory, 77
Bateson, Mary Catherine, 54
Bellah, Robert, 131 n. 3
belonging, sense of, 46–51
Berry, Wendell, 75, 76–77, 100
Bonhoeffer, Dietrich, 55, 74, 114
Book of Common Prayer, The, 76–77
Bridges, Ruby, 42–45
Buechner, Frederick, 58

call, four forms of, 104–5
calling, sense of, 52–58; in all Christians,
    56–57, 75–77, 125 n. 16; in daily work,
    56, 75, 125 n. 15; not self-actualization,
    55–56; and service, 56, 58; and
    worship, 69. *See also* vocation

Calvin, John, 63
Carroll, Jackson, 117 n. 2
Carson, Tom, 122 n. 4
children, 2, 44–45. *See also* adolescents
Christian Church (Disciples of Christ),
    117 n. 1
church: as a club, 62, 64, 73–74; as colony,
    126 n. 4; early Christian, 35, 86–87;
    finances, 73, 84, 85 (*see also* steward-
    ship); medieval imagery of, 63;
    pilgrim identity of, 22–26; restructur-
    ing, 2, 4, 13, 79–81, 119 n. 4; and search
    for meaning, 19, 62, 110; in the world,
    63–64, 74–75 (*see also* vocation). *See
    also* liberal Protestant tradition
church buildings, 22, 26. *See also* New
    England meeting houses
church membership: attracting, 9–10,
    67–69, 73, 112–13; growth/decline of, 1,
    117 n. 2, 118 n. 4
circuses, 68–69, 127 n. 4
Clements, Ronald, 120 n. 7
clergy. *See* ministry, ordained
clergy vestments, 67
clubs, churches as, 62, 64, 73–74
Coles, Robert, 42–45
colony imagery, 126 n. 4
Columba, Saint, 112
communion, 88, 89
congregations: as communities of faith,
    3, 113; leadership models for, 84 (*see
    also* leadership); programming in, 73,